SPOOKY
Oregon

*Tales of Hauntings, Strange Happenings,
and Other Local Lore*

Second Edition

RETOLD BY S. E. SCHLOSSER

ILLUSTRATED BY PAUL G. HOFFMAN

Globe Pequot

GUILFORD, CONNECTICUT

Globe
Pequot

An imprint of The Rowman & Littlefield Publishing Group, Inc.
4501 Forbes Blvd., Ste. 200
Lanham, MD 20706
www.rowman.com

Distributed by NATIONAL BOOK NETWORK

Copyright © S. E. Schlosser 2018

Illustrations by Paul G. Hoffman

British Library Cataloguing in Publication Information Available

Library of Congress Cataloging-in-Publication Data Available

ISBN 978-1-4930-3465-9 (paperback)
ISBN 978-1-4930-3466-6 (e-book)

∞™ The paper used in this publication meets the minimum requirements of American National Standard for Information Sciences—Permanence of Paper for Printed Library Materials, ANSI/NISO Z39.48-1992

Printed in the United States of America

*For my family: David, Dena, Tim, Arlene,
Hannah, Emma, Nathan, Ben, Deb, Gabe, Clare,
Jack, Chris, Karen, Davey, and Aunt Mil.*

For Cherrill Crosby and family. With my thanks.

*And for Mary Norris, Paul Hoffman, Jess Haberman, and
all the wonderful folks at Globe Pequot Press, with my thanks.*

*For Casey Schmitt, whose help in the archives
was invaluable. Many thanks.*

*My thanks to Dr. Daniel Wojcik for his permission to use
the Randall V. Mills Archive of Northwest Folklore.*

And for Chris Masoner, who shared his photos with me.

Contents

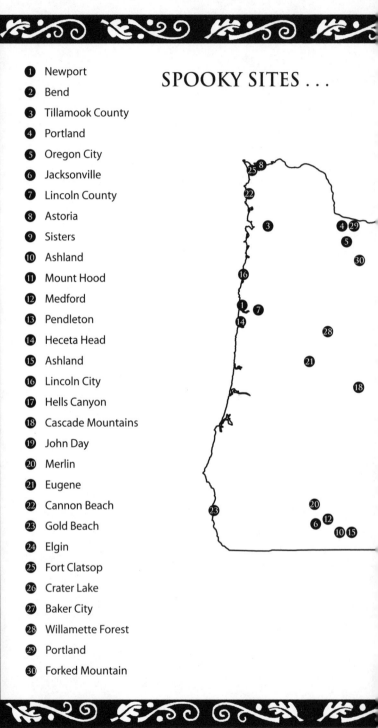

SPOOKY SITES . . .

1. Newport
2. Bend
3. Tillamook County
4. Portland
5. Oregon City
6. Jacksonville
7. Lincoln County
8. Astoria
9. Sisters
10. Ashland
11. Mount Hood
12. Medford
13. Pendleton
14. Heceta Head
15. Ashland
16. Lincoln City
17. Hells Canyon
18. Cascade Mountains
19. John Day
20. Merlin
21. Eugene
22. Cannon Beach
23. Gold Beach
24. Elgin
25. Fort Clatsop
26. Crater Lake
27. Baker City
28. Willamette Forest
29. Portland
30. Forked Mountain

AND WHERE TO FIND THEM

OREGON

Introduction

As I sat quietly on a bench, looking down over the Painted Hills of the John Day Fossil Beds, the spectacular red, tan, black, and gold colors that painted the landscape gleamed in the westering sunlight. In that moment, I fell in love with Oregon. Oh, I'd been oohing and aahing over the natural beauties of the state long before. From the lively streets of Portland to the lava beds atop the Cascade Mountains, I had admired Oregon as I traveled the state from end to end, meeting its residents and learning its folklore. But it was my visit to the Painted Hills that stole my heart away.

It was not just the beauty of the Oregon landscape that had impressed me on my journey. I liked her people, too. They had a tough-but-friendly spirit that drew me in. Many of them had descended from the men and women who dared to travel thousands of miles along the Oregon Trail to start a new life in the state's Willamette Valley (as told in the tale "Looking for Johnny"). Those determined pioneers crossed merciless deserts and tall mountains, wild rivers and steep cliffs, meeting every hardship with fortitude. Some of them left children behind, buried in the hard dirt beside the trail. Others left mothers or fathers. Those who survived thrived in their new home and were grateful for its bounty and beauty.

The good people of Oregon welcomed me wherever I traveled. One day I chanced upon a group of sixth graders while visiting the Lava Cave near Bend. They were on a class trip, studying the local geology, and they loved meeting a "Spooky" author. We sat down on the rocks near the entrance to the cave and teachers, parents, and students alike swapped ghost stories and talked and talked about what it was like to live in Oregon.

One of the first Oregon folktales they shared was an urban legend from Medford about a treacherous man who marries a woman with an unusual attribute—and murders her shortly after their marriage ("The Golden Hand"). We talked about the crimping trade in Portland—that is, the kidnapping of men to be sailors—and the folktales that had come along with it ("Shanghaied"). Then I shared one of my favorite spooky campfire tales—the one about an insane logger working on the Oregon Coast whose ghost hunts down and kills anyone who dares trespass on his territory ("The Mad Logger"). The student's eyes grew large and they giggled mischievously—and a little nervously. Finally, I took my leave and headed out to the little Wild West town of John Day, where miners once flocked to dig for gold and a *Bucca* once saved the life of a bloke caught in a cave-in ("Tommy Knockin'").

Looking back, I can't find enough superlatives to describe the state of Oregon. Amazing, beautiful, breathtaking! I've never traveled anywhere with such stunning vistas. There were seascapes that look much the same now as they did when first viewed by the intrepid explorers Lewis and Clark ("Time Slip"). And I am still awestruck when I think of the incredible rapids, deep gorges, and stunning mountains of Hells Canyon and the Snake River, with its mysterious lights and ghostly cemeteries ("The Lights").

And Crater Lake! Words can't describe the feeling of walking through fifteen-foot snowdrifts in my shirt sleeves, drinking in the deep, deep blue of the sacred lake with its mysterious Wizard Island. The lake is said to have once been home to the dark lord of the underworld ("Destiny").

Like its incredible scenery and the incredible people who populate it, Oregon is rich with folklore that is larger than life. It ranges from the sublimely mythological to the ultramodern. It encompasses many characters, from college students with supernatural abilities ("The Cheshire Cat") to insane mummies ("Bandage Man"); from headstrong children ("Neahkahnie Treasure") to gold-crazy placer-miners ("Laughing Devil"). There are griffins in Merlin, vampires in Baker City, and Bigfoot in more than one county. I hope you enjoy Oregon folklore as much as I do. And if you've never been to Oregon, just wait. You've got a treat in store!

—Sandy Schlosser

PART ONE
Ghost Stories

1

The Handkerchief

NEWPORT

She climbed the sand dune swiftly, giggling nervously at her daring, as the soft mist of an early evening fog swirled around her. The ocean waves boomed against the beach below her, and the wind slapped at her face, driving sand into her eyes as if it were warning her away. But she kept on climbing, though her feet slipped often in the shifting sand. Around her, her friends were scrambling through the sand and long grass, heading steadily upward toward the abandoned gray house that sat on the ridge between the sea and the harbor. The haunted lighthouse. At least, that's what some folks called it in town.

Muriel was new to Newport and had been bored with life until a group of vacationers arrived for the season. Many were as young as she was, and she delighted in their company and joined them as they explored tide pools and sea caves and sang around the campfire. When one of them suggested visiting the abandoned lighthouse, Muriel had felt a pang of warning inside her ribs. The weather-beaten home with a light perched at the top like an afterthought was the source of several stories around town. Folks said that mysterious lights sometimes appeared in its darkened windows, and that moans and shrieks could

THE HANDKERCHIEF

be heard coming from its top floors in the foggy hours just before a storm. They told Muriel that no one had ever died in the house, and that no one knew the source of the lights and sounds. Muriel laughed when she heard these stories, but she half-believed them, and the idea of visiting the lighthouse made her nervous.

Still, her friends wanted to go, and they had persuaded the caretaker of the lighthouse to loan them a key. So she went with them in spite of her misgivings. Now they were standing next to the rickety old fence that surrounded the building. Before them, the dilapidated, box-like structure with its creaky, crooked little porch and tall, ominous door loomed menacingly in the growing fog. Clouds had darkened the late afternoon sun, and the cracked windows of the house looked like black eyes peering menacingly down on the eager faces of the young people who dared to approach it.

Muriel gave a sudden shudder, her skin prickling apprehensively. One of the boys saw her shiver and jeered: "Afraid, Muriel?"

"I'm not," she replied, sticking out her chin. Even if she were afraid (and she was), she would never admit it in front of her chums. She seized the arm of her beau, Harold, and marched him right up to the door. Harold obediently produced the key, and in a few moments, the group was inside the dusty interior of the old house, staring around the front hallway and up the steep staircase. One or two of the girls giggled and started exploring the kitchen and the sitting rooms, while the boys peeked into the cellar.

In the dusk caused by the lowering clouds and the swirling fog, the gaping black mouth of the cellar was a bit too creepy for Muriel. She grabbed Harold by the hand and pulled him upstairs where there was more light. The stairs creaked and groaned under their weight, and Muriel shuddered. The abandoned house made her very uncomfortable. It was so bare, so empty of life—and yet full of strange moaning sounds caused by the wind whipping around the light above them. Muriel jumped when a loose shutter banged suddenly against the side of the house, and a couple of the other girls shrieked and then laughed shakily when they realized what had happened. Their voices echoed strangely.

Harold entered one of the front rooms, with Muriel right on his heels. He glanced around the room—too large without its furnishings—and then wandered up a second staircase and looked into a tiny room beside the metal steps leading up to the lantern tower. The room was no bigger than a linen cupboard, Muriel thought, looking over his shoulder. There came the sound of footsteps pounding up the staircase behind them. A moment later, the whole group was crowded into the small space.

"Ooh," moaned one of the girls in her best spooky voice. "Ooh! I am the ghost of this house. Leave now or die!" She waved her arms about in what was supposed to be a ghostly fashion. Muriel thought she looked stupid. One of the boys backed away from the "ghost" and bumped into the wainscoting on the wall. A piece of it broke off on impact.

"Now look what you made me do," said the boy, turning indignantly and catching the falling piece of wainscoting. "This place is falling apart!"

Then they saw it. An iron panel gleamed through the gap in the wall. The youth tapped the iron, and they all heard a hollow knocking sound ring through the cupboard. The sound filled Muriel with a sense of foreboding. *Nonsense*, she whispered silently.

"Let's see if we can move it," Harold said, and together the two boys removed the iron square, revealing a small crawl space with a gaping black hole in the bottom of it. Everyone gasped and took turns looking down into the dark space. One intrepid lad crawled inside and dropped pebbles down into the hole, but none of them heard them reach the bottom of the pit.

All the hair on Muriel's arms stood on end as she thought of smugglers crawling up the dark hole and into the uncanny old house. Or pirates stashing their ill-gotten gains in the empty rooms, waiting to load them aboard their ship. Anything or anyone might come up through such a hole. Her face flushed with fear and her arms grew cold.

Muriel pulled out her handkerchief with shaking fingers and wiped her suddenly sweaty forehead. "Let's get out of here," she said, backing away from the crawl space and starting toward the stairs. No one jeered at her this time. They were all frightened by the black hole inside the tiny room.

The light coming from the window opposite them was growing dim. And the fog outside was so thick that Muriel couldn't see anything through the window save the swirls of mist created by the sea winds.

"We haven't been up the tower yet," said Harold, catching her by the shoulder. Muriel swallowed her dread and nodded with what she hoped was a carefree smile. One by one, they climbed the ladder to the tower and looked out into the mist and growing darkness.

"You can't even see the ocean," complained the "ghost" girl. "This fog makes me feel lonesome. Let's go back to camp."

Thinking of the gaping black hole to nowhere below them, Muriel was quick to agree. It didn't take them long to swarm down the ladder, down two flights of creaky, worn stairs, and out into the foggy dusk. As Muriel stood beside Harold, watching him lock the door to the lighthouse, she reached again for her handkerchief to wipe away the telltale sweat of relief on her face and realized it was gone.

"Harold, I've left my handkerchief inside," she exclaimed. And wanted to bite her tongue. But it was too late. Gallantly, Harold volunteered to get it for her, and in his eyes she saw the same attitude held by the other boy who had teased her. To Harold, she was just a pretty little girl to be protected—or mocked. Muriel felt a sudden spurt of anger.

"No need. I'll fetch it myself and come out the kitchen door," she said carelessly, giving him a smile. Reluctantly, he let her into the house, and when she glanced back, she saw him waiting by the half-open front door. The sight stiffened her spine. She was not a helpless, pretty little thing. She was Muriel, almost a woman grown.

"You don't have to wait," she called angrily. "Lock the door and go on. I'll meet you down the hill."

She turned and marched up the staircase, not bothering to look back. Behind her, she heard the sound of the door snicking shut and the key turning. And that's when she realized she was alone in the drafty, dark, uncanny house. All alone. Dread seized her, and she wanted desperately to run. But what a fool she would look if she returned to the others without her handkerchief. Panting with terror, Muriel forced herself across the little landing and started up the second staircase toward the linen cupboard. She paused once, pulse pounding madly. Was that a thump she heard upstairs?

Don't be silly, she told herself, forcing her shaking legs up another step. *It's just the loose shutter blowing in the wind.* And then all the hair on the back of her neck stood on end as she realized she could hear something breathing behind her.

The boys and girls all came running back to the lighthouse when they heard her terrible screams, the last one a stifled cry for help. Harold wrenched and wrenched at the key until the door opened, and they ran through the house, frantically yelling for Muriel. But the house was deserted. Beside the linen cupboard and the iron ladder leading to the tower, they found a large pool of hot blood, still steaming in the cool air of the house. Beside it was a small, white handkerchief.

Muriel was never seen again.

2

Top Hat and Cane

BEND

Everyone in the neighborhood considered the man a bit strange. He'd come west long after it was settled, but before things had settled down. He always wore a black top hat and carried a fancy cane—not quite the style here in the wilds of Oregon. And though he carried himself like an English lord, he spoke with a Boston accent. Top Hat was looking for a place to live and finally settled on an old ranch just outside of town that had been vacated when the rancher who ran it went bankrupt.

As soon as the purchase was made, Top Hat went back east, collected his pretty wife, Margaret, and brought her first by train and then by wagon out to the little ranch in the middle of nowhere. Margaret immediately fell in love with the sagebrush and desert flowers of the Wild West. She was a delicate woman with blond curls and a pink mouth that was always smiling. When her blue eyes looked into yours, it sorta made you wish you were a better person.

Top Hat and Margaret settled down on the ranch, bought a couple of cows, and did their best to make a kitchen garden in the desert soil. Other than tending his horses and cattle, Top Hat didn't do much work. Folks figured he must have inherited money, though he never said one way or the other and no one ever asked. Top Hat was a secretive kind of person. He was plenty friendly when he stopped by the local store to pick up supplies or the smithy to have his horse shod. But he didn't encourage questions.

Folks in town liked to speculate about Top Hat around the pot-bellied stove in the mercantile during chilly winter evenings. The theories were as outlandish as Top Hat's clothes. He was a runaway ringmaster from the circus. An old-time attorney like Abe Lincoln. An English aristocrat sent to America to pay for his crimes. The list went on and on. The only thing folks agreed upon was that Top Hat had a gem of a wife and that he very rightly adored her. In the end, perhaps, he loved her too much.

About six months after Top Hat and Margaret settled outside of town, it became obvious that the little woman was in the family way. 'Round about Christmas, a boy was born, and there was much rejoicing—in town as well as at the ranch house. Some of the fellows joked that the boy should be given a top hat like his Pa, but the joking was all in good fun. Top Hat and Margaret blossomed out a bit socially, coming to a few of the local dances and church socials to show off their son. It was a happy time.

And it promised to be happier yet. Before two years had passed, Margaret was once again with child. But then tragedy struck. The little girl Margaret was expecting was stillborn, and Margaret herself died just a few hours later. The doc couldn't do anything to save her. He offered to get the minister or a couple of neighbors to come and stay with Top Hat and little Tommy, but the doctor's offer was gently but proudly turned aside. "We'll manage," said Top Hat, his face a mask behind

TOP HAT AND CANE

which the doctor sensed great pain. If only he had known how great, the doctor might not have left. "Please tell our friends that we'd like to be alone for a few days. I'll contact them about a funeral."

The doctor reported the death, and everyone in town was shocked and sorry. Respecting Top Hat's wish for privacy, the townsfolk waited for nearly two weeks for news of the funeral. When they didn't hear from Top Hat by then, the minister decided to break the silence. He loaded up his bag with homemade bread and pies and headed out to the bereaved man's ranch. The first thing he noticed when he turned down the lane was all of Top Hat's horses and cattle wandering here, there, and everywhere. Part of the fence had fallen down, and no one had fixed it. The minister began to feel uneasy. He pulled his wagon up next to the barn and called out a jolly greeting. No one answered. He dismounted and went into the open door of the barn, calling again for Top Hat. Then he stopped in alarm as a tall, dark shadow loomed above him, dangling from the tallest rafter. It was the bereaved husband—hatless for the first time in memory.

Stunned, the minister backed away from the gruesome, twisted face of the once handsome man. His first thought was to cut the man down. Then he remembered little Tommy. Leaving Top Hat in the barn, he rushed to the house, calling for the little toddler. There was no answer. The minister went into the front room and found it empty save for a top hat and cane carefully laid on a table by the front window. Beside it was a handmade rocking chair that Top Hat had made for his wife when he found out she was expecting their second child. But no Tommy.

The minister ran through each room on the ground floor and then upstairs, searching frantically. Finally, he climbed the staircase to the attic. There he found a beautiful, flowered bower carefully constructed in the center of the floor with the fair Margaret laid carefully out in her best dress. Huddled on the floor below his mother's corpse lay little Tommy. He was curled into a ball, and he wasn't breathing. Heart-stricken, the minister went back to the barn, cut down the poor husband, and laid him out with his dead family. Then he went to break the news to the folks in town.

The minister held a triple funeral the next day, instead of a single. And then the ranch house was carefully shut up until folks could trace Top Hat's heirs. Somehow, no one wanted to disturb the carefully constructed scene in the front room, so the house was left just as the minister had found it, with the top hat and cane visible through the front window facing the road, with the beautifully carved rocking chair standing beside them.

About a month after the death of the family, neighbors on either side of the ranch reported seeing strange lights hovering near the house and hearing strange sounds coming from the property at night. It got so that folks around town were downright spooked at the idea of passing Top Hat's ranch after dark. But the local butcher was a brave man, and he disregarded the rumors. After spending one Sunday visiting his mother across town, he decided to take a shortcut past Top Hat's abandoned ranch to get home in time to tend his livestock before bed.

As the butcher neared the abandoned ranch, he heard a faint grating sound through the pines on either side of the narrow road. It sounded like a rocking chair creaking softly as it moved back and forth. But that was nonsense! It must be the wind rubbing one old tree limb against another. Except there was no wind that night—not the faintest breeze.

When the butcher reached the lane leading to the abandoned house, he heard the sound of a little child wailing. Alarmed, the butcher reined in his horse. Had someone's child broken into the house and been hurt? The sound came again; a little boy whimpering in fear and dismay.

The butcher turned his horse down the lane and rode toward the ranch house. Then he pulled up abruptly, heart pounding. A blue light was glowing in the front window, highlighting the black top hat and cane. Beside them, the rocking chair was moving back and forth, back and forth, but no one was in it. The butcher's horse whinnied in alarm and thrashed its head up and down violently. The butcher felt shudders run up and down his whole body, and his heart thudded painfully. The child's wail came again, and a voice spoke gently: "Don't cry, baby. Mama's here." But there was no one there.

The butcher gave a shout of fear, and his horse bolted back the way they had come. Butcher and horse were drenched in sweat and trembling mightily when they arrived at the mercantile to report the strange happening to the men gathered there to play checkers. The story spread through town like wildfire. After that, folks with business out in that direction took the long way around rather than pass the haunted place.

No heirs for the ranch were ever located, and folks in the town government wanted nothing to do with the property. The house eventually fell into ruin and was torn down. But to this day, folks wandering outside town report seeing a blue light that sometimes takes on the shape of a tall man with a top hat and cane. And at dusk each night, they say, you can hear a child weeping.

3

Neahkahnie Treasure

TILLAMOOK COUNTY

My pal Nicky and I decided to go treasure hunting one night in late spring. I waited outside in the bushes while he climbed out his bedroom window with the treasure map, and then we grabbed the shovels and other tools we'd tucked into the woodshed that afternoon and took off for the coast on our bikes.

We'd heard the stories all our lives. How pirates had chased a Spanish schooner heavy with gold and silver and jewels up the coast from South America. At first it seemed that the schooner would escape the dread foe, but that was before it ran headlong into a massive storm along the coast. The waves towered above the beleaguered vessel, tossing it back and forth, side to side, up and down. First one and then a second mast broke, causing the ship to pitch yet more wildly. The ship finally ran aground off Neahkahnie Mountain. In pouring, pounding rain, the frantic crew carried as much of the treasure as they could off the vessel as it was pummeled to pieces by the thunderous ocean waves. There they buried it in a secret place somewhere on the shores at the foot of the mountain. After the storm, when the pirates anchored their ship and rowed their tenders up beside the wrecked one, they found not one galleon of gold in its hull.

NEAHKAHNIE TREASURE

Infuriated, the pirates tracked down the shipwrecked crew and killed them, one by one, in a foul and torturous way, trying to pry the secret out of them. But not one of them would betray the whereabouts of the treasure, and the pirates never found it.

Only one person—the first mate of the treasure ship— escaped the pirates. The poor fellow survived only a year after the shipwreck before falling ill with smallpox. On his deathbed, he drew a map for the loving family who had taken him in after the shipwreck, in gratitude for their kindness. And the map had been handed down in that family—Nicky's family—ever since. People in every generation had attempted to find the treasure, without success. But everyone was sure there was a secret to the map that—if solved—would make them wealthy beyond their dreams.

Nicky had spent most of his life trying to get a look at the family map. He was an ace at puzzles of all sorts, and I was an honor student often called a genius by the teachers at school. Between the two of us, we were convinced that we would be the ones to solve the family mystery. But his father kept the map in a safe-deposit box at the bank, and Nicky had never even got a glimpse of it.

Then our luck changed. Nicky's father brought the map home to show to a visiting uncle, and Nicky had swiped it during the night and made a copy of it on the family printer before returning it to his father's study. Since then, we'd spent every free moment studying the map, and Nicky showed me all the places other family members had tried digging, without success, in the years since the map had come into their possession.

As I frowned down at the map for what felt like the fortieth time, something stirred in my mind. For some reason, it didn't look like a map to me. The fir tree was jagged, as if it were made up of two or three unrelated parts. And the rocks and other markers didn't seem terribly connected to one another. In fact, the whole map looked more like one of those picture puzzles you see in the logic books. I mentioned this impression to Nicky, and his eyes grew wide. Then he grabbed a piece of paper and started sketching out the various pieces of the map. He tore them apart, and we both began arranging and rearranging them until we had a picture in front of us that we both recognized. A picture, not of a large tree and big rock, as were originally portrayed, but of a small sea cave surrounded by jagged rocks in a pattern we both knew very well. We'd been playing in that cave ever since we were little kids!

We made good time on our bikes, even carrying our clunky shovels and spades. It wasn't long before we heard the endless swell of the sea rolling against the shore. We tucked our bikes into a thicket of trees and climbed down the pathway to the rocky tide pools and the beach. The tide was out and the moon was full, both of which made walking easier as we picked our way to the little cave tucked into the cliff. It was more of a cleft than a cave—just a long indent with a curious crag shaped almost like a face jutting out above it.

Nicky turned on a big flashlight and tucked the end between two rocks so it shone brightly against the roof of the small indent. Then we both started digging, discussing in hushed but excited voices how we were going to carry away all the treasure. Maybe we should just carry some of it home tonight, enough to prove to our parents that we'd found it, and then come back for the rest in the morning. It was not easy work, digging in that sandy, rocky spot. Suddenly, my shovel hit something hard, and I gasped in excitement, trying to dig around it. I stopped abruptly. I'd hit solid rock, not a treasure chest. A few more minutes of digging showed that rock was under all the sand, spreading out everywhere with no crevices, no possible place for treasure to lie buried.

I sank abruptly to the sandy floor, devastated. Nicky kept digging awhile in various spots, too stubborn to admit I was right. Then he too sank down with his back against the far wall. And disappeared.

I gave an astonished yell and started to my feet. Then Nicky reappeared in the cave, his eyes huge with astonishment. "Come here," he said, beckoning to me with shaking hands. I caught up the flashlight and walked over to the seemingly solid wall. And found the gap Nicky had fallen through. It was completely hidden from view, unless you stood or sat in just the right spot. And even then it was impossible to see until you were inches from the crevice. I stepped through and found the opening wider than I thought. *A bit of an optical illusion*, I mused, and then stared as the flashlight revealed row upon row of dark trunks lined up in the small chamber. The Neahkahnie Treasure.

It was at this moment that the moaning began. It came both from behind and ahead of me. At least that's what I heard. Nicky later claimed that he heard it coming from directly overhead. Wherever it came from, it was a sound that made the hairs on my arms and legs stand on end and my whole body shake from head to toe. It was the sound of many voices at once, each moaning on a slightly different pitch. The moans seemed to be wrung from throats tortured beyond bearing, too weak even to scream. Cold shivers ran across my shoulders as small pinpricks of light like fireflies started flickering on and off around the chamber, lighting up the treasure chests and revealing Nicky's too-pale face and the look of terror in his dark eyes.

Suddenly, a blaze of blue-white fire sprang up in front of the treasure chests, and a flaming figure in the clothes of an old-time mariner drew a cutlass and pointed it first at Nicky and then at me. More dead sailors appeared as the firefly lights grew thicker. The menace in the air made it hard to breathe, but I stood my ground. Nicky glanced at my determined face and stood with me.

"We aren't pirates," I said bravely to the dead sailors, though my voice shook with the effort. "We were given a map by your first mate. He wanted us to have the treasure."

I don't know what I expected. In films, the brave hero wins the day and gains the treasure. He doesn't suddenly find himself grabbed from behind by skeletal hands and overwhelmed by the stench of death and decay.

"If you want our treasure," a voiceless whisper hissed in my mind, "you must become one of us!"

Nicky shrieked in terror as a skeleton wearing the rotted garb of a Spanish sailor grabbed his arms and dragged him backward through the crevice into the outer sea cave. I shouted and kicked and struggled against the one holding me, finally managing to dislodge it by dropping to the floor of the cave, half in the treasure chamber and half out of it. The treasure room went white with a blinding blaze of light, filled with a deafening roar from the dead sailors who guarded it. I ran for my life, striking the skeleton holding Nicky and grabbing his arm to drag him out of the cave and away down the shore toward our bikes.

I don't really remember the ride home. I dropped a trembling, panting Nicky off by his toolshed and raced home as fast as I could go. It was only after I was in bed, under the covers, that I realized we'd left the shovels back in the cave.

Nicky and I waited until high noon the next day to return to the sea cave to retrieve his dad's tools. But when we entered the little cove where the sea cave stood, we couldn't find it. The needle-sharp rocks that marked the entrance to the cave were still there, but the long indent with the curious crag above it was gone. The disappearance frightened us even more than the ghosts had. How could a sea cave in which we'd played all our lives vanish? We ran pell-mell for home, and Nicky burned the photocopies of the map. And that was the last time we ever searched for buried treasure.

4

Shanghaied

PORTLAND

The boy had to go. There was no doubt in my mind about that. When I married his mother five years ago, he was still young enough to obey me, and that was all I required. But insubordination was something I was not willing to tolerate. And lately the boy had begun to question me at every turn.

Still, it would not do to alienate his mother, of whom I was very fond. Especially now that she was expecting our first child. I had suggested sending the boy to private school, or finding him an apprenticeship in some faraway spot, but his mother wouldn't hear of her beloved child leaving the nest so soon.

Some "child." He was a good fourteen years old, a sulky, red-headed youth with a fierce temper and rebellious ways. Whenever we fought—which was almost daily—his mother sided with her "little boy" and told me I was too harsh with him. Once he dared defy me in front of my dinner guests, and that night I took my cane and beat him. My wife was furious with me and threatened to leave. Why was she so blind to the boy's faults?

Finally, I hit upon a plan. The birth of my child would make the boy ill at ease and make him jealous. It would be just like the misfit to "run away" to sea to frighten his poor mother into continuing her favoritism. Which, of course, she would not do once she held my perfect little boy in her arms. Knowing my wife, she would melt like butter over the baby and hardly notice that her son had disappeared.

I waited until the night my wife went into labor. Then I called the sulky boy into my study and offered him a drink, claiming that I wished for us to put the bad blood behind us now that there would be a small child in the house for us to look after. I sounded horribly maudlin, and pompous to boot. But the silly boy bought it and eagerly gulped down the large glass of whiskey I offered him like it was water. I handed him another and then another, encouraging him to talk as he drunk himself into a stupor. Foolish talk it was, too, about his plans to be a famous writer or a newspaperman like Mark Twain, covering the gold rush and other important happenings all over the United States. *What a worthless ambition*, I thought, as I topped off his glass. There was no helping some boys.

Soon enough he toppled back into his chair in a drunken stupor. And I crept into the front parlor to watch for the crimping wagon, which usually passed our home about this time of night. The crimpers made a good living in this town, kidnapping drunken miners and workmen who frequented the local taverns and selling them to sea captains who needed a crew to man their vessels. By the time the poor drunken fools woke up, they were imprisoned in the hold of the ship and were often so far off to sea that they had no choice but to stay and work as sailors until the ship returned to Portland—which could take several years if the ship were bound for Shanghai.

I lurked in the front parlor, watching out the window, until I saw the familiar wagon headed my way. Then I raced outdoors, calling out to the driver: "Bunco! Bunco Kelly. Wait a moment." Bunco Kelly, one of the most prominent crimpers in Portland, turned to me enquiringly.

"And how are you this fine evening, Jeremiah?" he asked politely, recognizing me from my visits to a pub we both frequented.

"My wife's giving birth to my first child," I said proudly. "By tomorrow I'll have a son!"

"Could be a girl," Kelly suggested, but I brushed aside this nonsense. Of course it would be a son.

"I have a guest for your wagon," I said, changing the subject to the one foremost in my mind. "A young fellow who has proved himself too much of a nuisance for his own good."

Bunco Kelly nodded understandingly. He was a hardened fellow who had once found a group of twenty-two men dying in a cellar after drinking embalming fluid in the mistaken belief that it was hard liquor. Rather than helping them, he'd sold every last one to a desperate sea captain seeking a crew. Apparently, they all died aboard ship before they even made it up the river to the town of Astoria on the coast. A man who would do something like that wouldn't blink an eye at a fellow trying to sell his own stepson to the sea.

Within a moment, the deal was done, and Bunco Kelly himself carried the drunken boy out of the house and dumped him in the crimping wagon with the other poor fools heading— unbeknownst—to Shanghai. I went back to my study, cleaned up the evidence of the drinking session, and then composed a note—supposedly from the boy to his mother—stating his ire that she should have another child and telling her he'd run away to sea.

SHANGHAIED

I almost wished the boy back the next morning when the doctor informed me that my wife had delivered a mewling, yellow-skinned, whiny girl-child instead of the expected son. At least with the boy around I had a son—of sorts. But the deed was done. And when my wife, heartbroken after reading the note I had composed, lost her child a week later to some common-as-muck infant disease, she took to her bed and didn't rise again for a month. Then she haunted the docks for a time, asking the dockhands if anyone could tell her which ship her boy had "signed on" to and where it was bound. But no one could.

I had been careful in my note to lay the root cause of the boy's disappearance squarely upon his mother's pregnancy, yet still she blamed me for the loss. A coolness lay between us for many months. But time heals these things. We finally reconciled and eventually my wife found herself with child again—and almost happy. A year had passed since the boy had "gone away," and she was counting the days when his ship would return and she would see him again. I had no intention of telling her what I had told Bunco Kelly—that I wanted the boy on a ship to

Shanghai, with no way for him to return for the next three to five years.

Time passed swiftly and enjoyably, for me at least, without the rebellious boy. Then my pride and joy was born—a son, at last! My cup ran full over. At least it did until one night when I was awakened by the sound of a low moaning that grew louder and louder until it filled the bedroom. My blood ran cold, and I hastened to light a lamp with shaking hands. But my groping hand knocked the lamp to the floor, and I was left alone in the dark with a terrible moaning that rang through the room and buzzed in my head until it ached. I clapped my hands over my ears, glad that my wife was still safely sleeping in the nursery with my new son.

Then I realized that the room was no longer dark. A ball of light appeared, floating at the foot of the broad bed. It began to twist and writhe, and I blinked rapidly, trying to ease the prickling ache the light caused in my eyes. The light was growing large, and forming into a shape that—heart thumping—I recognized. It was the figure of my stepson, still on a ship to Shanghai. Or so I thought he was—until this moment, when I saw his ghost, and realized he was dead. The ghost was hung with seaweed, its face bloated and blue. It pointed a finger at me and cried: "He is the one. He is the one who sent me to my death at sea."

It seemed a strange thing to say, as if he were speaking to someone else. And that's when I saw the other white figure standing in the doorway. It was my wife, holding the baby in her arms and staring at me with a look of utter betrayal upon her face, made all the more awful by the incandescent light of the ghost. For a long moment we stared at one another. I tried to call her name, but my throat was still choked with dread, and all I could do was sputter. Then she turned on her heel and left, and the ghost gave a shout of triumph and vanished with her.

By the time I could stop my legs shaking well enough to walk, my wife had wrapped up the baby in a blanket and left the house. In a panic I searched the hotels and inns that dotted our town, but to no avail. My wife had no family in the area, and I had never bothered to learn the names of her particular friends, so I had no real idea where she might be. Finally, near daylight, I went home to lock myself in my study and drink away my sorrows.

I awoke a long time later, feeling stiff and sore and hung over. And for some reason, I found I couldn't move. I was bumping along in a wagon, and, I noticed with increasing alarm, my hands and feet were tied behind my back. The driver noticed my thrashing and leaned over the side of the wagon, beaming at me with sardonic delight.

"This is just a little present to you from your wife," said Bunco Kelly. "A nice, long voyage at sea! Now isn't that nice?" He laughed and called out to his horses. And above his voice I heard, coming ever closer, the unmistakable lapping of the river against the docks of the harbor.

Looking for Johnny

OREGON CITY

It seems like I've spent all my life looking for Johnny, I thought to myself as I wandered into the front parlor with my knitting. That rascal of a son of mine was always disappearing here and there on his own business.

I frowned a little as I looked around the room. It wasn't arranged the way I remembered. The furniture was strange and modern, the curtains were the wrong color, and I had never in my life seen those shades. I touched the one on the front window and it snapped up at once. *Better,* I thought, as I settled down on a flower-covered easy chair next to the window where I could see the front walk. As I knitted, I kept a lookout for my boy. It was close to suppertime, and he should be coming back from the barn any minute now. I expected him to try to wheedle a piece of apple pie out of me even though supper was almost ready.

I smiled as I thought about my curly-haired, brown-eyed boy, so like his father. I'd started looking for Johnny as soon as he could crawl. That boy could disappear in a flash, crawling under the big kitchen table while I peeled potatoes, wandering into cupboards while I shucked corn, and sneaking out the back door onto the porch while I pumped water to heat on the old stove. He even tried to crawl up and down the stairs, tumbling more than once before I knew he was there. It's a wonder he lived to walk.

But walk he did, and then I was busy looking for Johnny upstairs in his room or down behind the big barn with the horses or at the creek getting his clothes all wet splashing in the shallow water with the dog. When he was a schoolboy, I'd find him playing at the neighbor-boy's house or climbing trees in the woods or buying sweets at the local store—all when he was supposed to be doing his chores. That boy was everywhere.

When Johnny turned eight, my husband sold the house and packed the three of us into a wagon heading west on the Oregon Trail. We left from Independence with a medium-size wagon train. At least, the folks in Independence called it medium size. To me, it looked as if the white-topped wagons extended for miles! I was amazed at how many folks were heading to the Willamette Valley. Teddy had painted "Bound for Oregon" in huge letters on our cover, which made our wagon stand out from the others in our party.

Day after long day, we found ourselves bumping along inside an uncomfortable covered wagon. It was so uncomfortable that Johnny and I spent more of our time walking than riding, only climbing aboard the wagon on rainy days when the constant dripping and wet clothing were harder to bear than the bumps. Three days into our trip, I decided to try an experiment. After milking our cow in the morning, I filled the churn with cream and put it in back of the jiggling, bumping wagon. By nightfall, it had turned to butter! I made butter that way for the rest of the trip.

LOOKING FOR JOHNNY

At first we enjoyed ourselves. Each morning, we got up at four o'clock and did chores. Johnny helped me fetch water, cook, clean dishes, and pack, while Teddy tended the livestock, hunted for food, and made repairs. Then the wagons moved out in a long line along the Santa Fe Trail. We were fortunate that first month: the weather was fair, the trail was well-worn, and walking was pleasant. We generally followed the path of least resistance, skirting hills and weaving through washes and valleys, tracing paths used for centuries by the Indians. Sometimes I'd drive our wagon so Teddy could walk or barter with the Indians or do a round of guard duty. I'd heard there was one death for every person who walked this long trail, but in the first few weeks of travel, I found it hard to believe.

During this time, we got to know our fellow emigrants well. We women enjoyed chatting with one another and planning out our new homes in Oregon while our children raced and shouted and played together. I was always looking for Johnny then, to make sure he didn't fall under a wagon wheel or get lost on the prairie or shoot off his father's rifle while playing in the back of the wagon. But he was a sturdy fellow and remained relatively unscathed, save for a near miss with a snake once in the tall grass.

In this manner, we traveled through Nebraska, following the Great Platte River Road. It was not unusual to hear someone calling out "he's stumped" along the way as an unlucky driver broke an axle against a rock or a tree stump. Luckily, our wagon remained free of accidents, due in great part to Teddy's careful driving. One day, we saw Chimney Rock on the horizon, and we watched all day as it loomed closer and closer, looking like a sweet potato with a pile of rocks rising out of its top. Then we veered south around Scotts Bluff, which my husband Teddy thought looked like a "grand old fort." Johnny laughed at this description and spent the rest of the afternoon pretending to be a soldier.

That evening, just before we halted for the night, the ground started shaking. Everyone looked up in panic, thinking it was an earthquake, and the wagon in front of us, already unbalanced on the path, tipped over. A cloud of dust billowing over a small rise was the only warning we had. Suddenly, a huge herd of buffalo came stampeding through the long grass, coming right toward the wagon train. In a second, all was chaos. Horses and oxen panicked. Women and children screamed and ran for the uncertain safety of the wagons. Dogs barked and hid under the wagons. That seemed like a good idea to me. I grabbed hold of Johnny and threw us both under the wagon, yelling for Teddy to do the same. But he was too busy trying to hold the horses. The stampeding buffalo veered to the right when they saw the long line of covered wagons and streamed past us on one side. A few of the more intrepid beasts ran between the wagons, and several men shot at them, hoping to get a good meal or three for their families.

By the time the stampede had passed, wagons were overturned, many horses and cattle had run away with the herd, and one man had been dragged to his death when he got tangled in his panicking horse's reins. And there were other deaths. Two women, five children, and one old man had been trampled, and another man had been shot when a bullet missed a bison and hit him square in the heart. It was a disaster. We camped for three days in that place, fixing broken wagons, burying the dead, and trying to retrieve our runaway horses and cattle. Finally, heartsick and weary, the wagon train limped onward to Fort Laramie.

It was after this stop that things became really difficult. We were traveling in Wyoming over hot, sandy, stony roads. The weary animals found it harder and harder to pull the heavy wagons, and a piece at a time, folks began throwing away the luxuries they'd packed. Anvils, tools of every kind, sacks of flour and beans, tents, buckets, stoves, all cast off. Johnny loved looking at the abandoned items, wandering too far away from his Mama for her comfort. I spent a lot of time watching to make sure he didn't get lost or hurt as he played "let's pretend" with the objects he encountered on the trail.

We reached the mountains then and rejoiced when we saw Independence Rock looming over us like a giant whale. Teddy painted all our names on the rock in wagon grease to show the world we'd been there. A few miles later, we saw the Devil's Gate, and Johnny and I trotted over to take a look, leaving Teddy behind because the canyon was too narrow to travel through with the wagons. It was a beautiful spot.

I was so happy the day we crossed the Continental Divide at South Pass. We were halfway to Oregon! We stopped for the night at Pacific Spring and drank our fill of the very first Pacific-bound water in our journey. That night, after unhitching the horses, gathering firewood, and feeding the livestock, Teddy arranged for us to have a square dance after supper with some of our closest friends. Teddy got out his fiddle, a friend of ours played the jug, and the leader of the wagon train tried his hand with the harmonica. It was the most fun we'd had in weeks!

We traveled up to Fort Bridger, then down the Bear River Valley. And then, oh, my! We hit the Snake River, along which we would travel for three hundred more miles. The Snake was an awesome sight: wild and untamable, and infamous for its deep holes, unexpected surges, and terrible rapids. *How would we ever get across*, I wondered. But we still had a long way to go before we faced that crossing.

What can I say about the Snake River region? It was a dry, dusty, hot place, and everything in it seemed burnt. Even Johnny's high spirits flagged as we walked and walked along the river day after endless day. Our trail was full of sagebrush, and heat seemed to radiate from the volcanic bluffs around us. Dust got into everything: horses, food, people. I had to keep a sharp eye out for Johnny now, because rattlers were numerous. One of our oxen was bitten by one and died the same day. One of Johnny's little friends also died of a rattler bite, and Johnny himself was bitten by a scorpion and lay sick in the rattling bed of the wagon for three days. I was never as relieved as when he recovered! The road was so rocky in places it was almost impassable. And the path was often so narrow, and so covered with dung, that we could barely walk. We lost many horses and oxen along this passage, and the smell of death and dying daily made me retch.

We had to wait in line for days when we finally reached the Three Islands Ford. Teddy used the time to reinforce the caulking on our wagon and trade with the Indians for fresh fish. It made a nice change in our diet. Johnny loved watching his Pa bartering with the local tribesmen, and he went around for days calling: "How swap? How swap? Salmon for shirt!" Then our turn came. We lashed everything we could into the wagon bed, put the rest in rented canoes, and paid some of the Indians to swim our cows, horses, and oxen across after us. Hanging tightly to a rope, we pulled ourselves across the ford hand over hand, praying the whole way. Johnny thought it was fun. I most emphatically did not!

That was quite a time, I thought to myself, returning to my knitting and the present time while glancing out the front window again for Johnny. Suddenly I saw a strange-looking man and what I took to be a boy with long, blond hair coming up the front walk. Their clothes were most peculiar, and I suddenly realized the boy was actually a girl wearing trousers! I hurried to the front door and opened it, staring at my strange guests. To my indignation, the boyish-looking girl walked right past me without a glance and went up the front staircase. The man stood like a buffoon on the front porch and stared at me, as white as a sheet. Then he edged inside and almost ran into the kitchen, slamming the door behind him. Well, really! *People are so rude*, I thought, glancing in both directions to see if Johnny had come back from the barn. There was no sign of him, so I went back to my knitting and my memories.

I first saw the Blue Mountains after we passed Flagstaff Hill. They were snow-capped wonders heavily forested with pines and other evergreen trees. They were glorious to behold, but my heart grew heavy at the sight. How were we ever to cross those heights? As we camped that night in the Powder River Valley, frost formed on our wagons. This in August! The next morning, we encountered some traders who had just come from the Willamette Valley—our future home. Teddy found this encouraging. We were nearly there.

Over the next few weeks, we hacked our way up and over the mountains, using axes to cut through the thick timber. We were forced to haul our wagons up slopes that were nearly vertical in places. It took twenty-two oxen to pull a single wagon in some spots! Narrow passages in the trail required careful maneuvering, and we were often forced to double-team on the ascents and break for one another on the descents. Each morning I had to crack the ice on the water bucket before we could wash up and dress. I thought we would never make it over those treacherous mountains, but we did.

I heaved a sigh of relief the day we emerged onto the Columbia plateau, though walking through the sandy plains was no respite. We were plagued by cruel winds, tumbleweeds, and sandstorms as we traveled ever westward. It was tough going, especially with our worn-out teams and battered wagons. But weary, hungry, and footsore, we finally made it to the Dalles.

At the Dalles, we had two paths to choose from on our way to the Willamette Valley. There was the Barlowe Road over Mount Hood, which meant more forest and snow as well as bitter cold and mud. The other trail led down the treacherous Columbia River with her swiftly flowing waters and the mighty rapids within the gorge. Teddy took one look at Mount Hood and decided we were going on the river.

We weren't the only settlers who decided to chance the river when they learned that the west end of the gorge was wretchedly unsuitable for a wagon road, hemmed in as it was by cliffs and steep slopes. We didn't have enough money to buy a raft from the Hudson Bay Company, so Teddy made us one from pine logs, and we loaded our wagon onto it. We set off in company with a few other settlers who had been in our wagon train, hoping that we would make it safely through the awesome Columbia rapids.

Before the Dalles, the Columbia had been a rapid, shallow, and narrow river. Here it became wide, deep, and still and ran between precipitous, rocky banks that were as high as several hundred feet. As we floated further down the river, we came to an immense pile of loose rocks over which the water ran with great rapidity for six miles. Those swirling rapids made the trip down the Columbia treacherous, and I kept a firm eye on Johnny, who was pretending to be a sailor. Just to be safe, I tied a rope to his suspenders. That rope saved his life when our wagon hit a whirlpool, and Johnny was pitched out into the rushing water, as was one of the boys in a neighboring boat. We hauled Johnny out of the water as quickly as possible, but no one could reach the other boy, who drowned. Johnny was bruised and shaking, but alive. He recovered his spirits faster than his Mama did!

We had to portage our way around a truly immense set of Cascades, and then took to the river again. We finally reached Fort Vancouver with most of our belongings and our whole family intact. By this time, I was more than ready to leave the Columbia behind me. After the perils of the Santa Fe Trail, the last few miles along the Willamette Valley to Oregon City were a blessed relief. Following his dunking in the river, Johnny stayed close to me and Teddy, for which I was grateful. We came to our new hometown at long last, and Teddy went right out and bought us some farmland. Our new neighbors were friendly and helpful, and soon we were installed in our new house. Our journey was over at last.

Finishing off the last row of my knitting, I sighed happily and then frowned when the strange man peeked out of the kitchen door. He looked straight at me but didn't say a word. He didn't even seem to see me. He called out a woman's name—was it Sheila?—and then hurried upstairs. I hoped he'd had the decency to take the apple pie out of the oven before it burned. I realized then that I couldn't smell the apple pie, and I should have by now. Had I forgotten to put it in?

I looked out the window for Johnny, feeling uneasy. Something about this room, so familiar in size and shape, but not in furnishings, was making my head spin. I glanced down at my hands, glowing white and translucent, and tried to think. I was looking for Johnny. He was out in the barn doing his chores. Wasn't he?

A small voice at the back of my mind whispered that Johnny had died of smallpox a month after we settled in the Willamette Valley, more than a hundred years ago, that he was buried under the tree in the backyard. Right next to me.

The knitting needles hit the solid floor with a metallic thump. And I vanished.

6

The Green Lady

JACKSONVILLE

When we were first married, we rented a cottage at the back of a big estate called the Old House. It was a grand place—a mansion really—built back in the days of the gold rush when everyone came west to make their fortune. The couple who built the Old House really did strike it rich in the mountains and had settled here in Jacksonville. That was a couple of generations back. By the time we moved into the cottage, the last of the family line—a single daughter who never married—was the sole occupant of the Old House. She was a little thing, wrinkled and bent over, but very sweet. Everyone knew her, for she came to all the town activities and attended the local church faithfully. She still had a few servants to help around the house: a gardener and a housemaid and a cook.

Madam, as the townsfolk called her, loved to wander in the garden. She would stop sometimes by the cottage fence where I tended my rose bushes, and we'd talk for hours, always ending up inside my kitchen drinking tea and giggling like a pair of schoolgirls, in spite of a forty-year gap in our ages.

We were sitting around the table one hot summer afternoon when Madam asked me: "Do you believe in ghosts?" I was startled by the question. I'd asked her about the portrait of the lady in the long green dress that stood at the top of the main staircase in her home, and instead of answering my question, she asked me this.

"No, I don't," I said cautiously.

"I do," Madam said calmly. "The woman in the portrait is a ghost. She wanders the hallways of the manor just prior to the death of a family member. My father saw her just before his father died, and he saw her again when Mama passed away. She's called the Green Lady. Apparently, she was a daughter of the house who died in a boating accident long ago. Ever since then, she's haunted the manor."

"Did you ever see her?" I asked, trying not to sound skeptical. Madam nodded. "I saw her once, a long time ago, now. She came through the wall and floated down the hall, right before my eyes. She was wearing the same green dress she's wearing in the portrait. Two weeks later, my father died."

All this talk of death and dying made me nervous. I changed the subject by offering Madam more tea. The talk then turned to our summer plans, and the old lady flushed excitedly when she told me she was opening up the mansion for a big dance and that my husband and I were at the head of her guest list. That was enough to keep us talking until it was time to start supper, and I happily related the invitation to my husband later that night.

The manor was abuzz for days before the big event, with gardeners clipping and mowing and cutting outside, extra maids hired to turn out the house stem to stern, and the cook and caterers making delicacies long into the night.

Finally, the big day arrived. All afternoon, grand carriages and small handcarts, horses and buggies, and even a few of the

THE GREEN LADY

new-fangled automobiles made their way to the manor. I spent two solid hours primping until my husband finally dragged me next door. There was entertainment enough to suit every fancy. Lawn games for the adults, and a fun fair for the children. A woman had been hired to sing fancy songs for guests wandering inside the mansion, while a merry band played outside on the lawn. And the buffet was amazing! A few honored guests were invited to a separate sit-down meal in the early evening, while the majority kept on feasting at the buffet. My husband and I sat on either side of Madam as if we were her honored son and daughter.

When dessert was cleared away, Madam looked tired. "I'm going to have a short lie-down, my dear," she whispered to me. "While everyone is dancing. I'll be back down in time to say goodnight."

I gave the old woman a hug and watched as she hobbled up the great staircase toward her room on the second floor. Then my husband pulled me into the big ballroom and we danced and danced among the many happy couples. An hour into the dance, someone stepped on the ruffle of my dress, and it ripped right along the hem, hanging down dreadfully and getting in the way of my feet. Excusing myself, I ducked out of the ballroom and raced upstairs toward one of the bedrooms that had been set aside for the use of the female guests.

As I walked past Madam's room, the glowing figure of a woman stepped out of the wall in front of me and floated down the hallway. It was the woman in the portrait at the top of the stairs—the Green Lady! I froze in shock and fear when I saw her.

At that moment, Gladys, Madam's maid, turned the corner, pushing a tea trolley before her. The ghost walked right through the trolley and right through Gladys. Gladys gave a shriek of sheer terror and fainted, and the Green Lady disappeared through the wall at the end of the hall.

All this happened so quickly that I had no time to breathe. My whole body had stiffened in shock when I first saw the ghost, and now it started to tremble as I ran down the hall, tripping on my ripped ruffle, to see if Gladys was all right.

She was pale, but her pulse was strong. I pulled smelling salts out of my handbag and waved them under her nose until she awoke. Immediately Gladys burst into tears, wringing her hands and crying: "Oh, Missus, it was a ghost! I saw it! I turned the corner and the Green Lady walked right through me, just like that! Icy cold, she was. It gave me such a turn."

I shuddered at the thought of a ghost walking through me as Gladys pulled her clean, white apron over her head with a little wail. I helped her up and took her down to the kitchen for a cup of tea. Then I hurried upstairs to check on Madam. The old lady was just waking up from her nap and was happy to have my assistance as she readied herself for her guests. Then we went downstairs, and Madam joined her guests in one final dance before sending everyone off with her blessing.

I said my farewells and followed my husband back to the cottage, lost in thought. Dare I tell Madam about the Green Lady? Surely not. How do you ask someone if they've seen a ghost that may very well be foretelling their death? And the thought of Madam dying was too upsetting to contemplate.

In the end, I didn't have to say a word. Gladys said it for me, with trimmings. The story ran all around the village in the days following the party, taking on an enormous amount of detail that I myself did not remember. Gladys was treated as a sort of hero, and I saw her nearly every day down at the post office or the grocery, regaling folks with the story of the terrible ghost who was chased away by the intrepid housemaid. Of Madam, there was no sign, and I grew worried. Had something happened?

A week after the party, Madam appeared once again at my gate. Relieved, I ran down to greet her and ushered her into my kitchen. She was a little pale, but otherwise her manner was reassuringly the same. We laughed and talked as usual, and no mention was made of the Green Lady until the end of our visit. Madam gave me an unexpected hug and kiss as she turned to go, and said: "I probably won't see you again, my dear. The Green Lady is never wrong. You take good care of yourself, and I want you to name the baby after me!"

She disappeared along the garden path before I could utter a word. I stood gaping after her. How had she known about the baby? Even my husband didn't know yet. But I was more disturbed by her conviction that the visit of the Green Lady heralded her death. I hoped that she was wrong.

Exactly fourteen days after the party, Madam was found dead in her bed; she had suffered a heart attack, the doctor said. No one was really surprised to hear the news after the ghostly sighting a fortnight before. But there was one thing that confused people. The giant portrait of the Green Lady was found propped at the foot of Madam's bed on the morning of her death, and no one knew how it got there. The tiny Madam certainly could not have lifted it from its place on the wall.

Seven months after Madam's death, I gave birth to a little girl. We named her after Madam.

7

The Mad Logger

LINCOLN COUNTY

Of course, we're not *supposed* to go to the abandoned logging camp. Our parents would read us the riot act if they knew. So Billy and I told them we were going camping in one of the state parks, and they accepted our story.

And we *were* going camping, after all. It just so happened that we were going camping at the old logging site. The one that had been destroyed by a forest fire. The one that was supposedly haunted.

Billy's already got his driver's license, so we went in his car. We packed a big tent and lots of food and everything into our knapsacks. We were just going for the weekend, but the way our sacks bulged as we locked up the car and staggered into them, you'd think we were hiking across America. We laughed as we set off on the trails leading up and into the forest.

'Course, we weren't laughing so much a few hours later. Those backpacks were heavy! But we didn't want to leave anything behind, so we trudged on. To take our minds off our load, we started discussing our destination in low tones, almost as if we were afraid of being overheard—which was ridiculous. After all, we were in the middle of one of the nation's gorgeous

forests, surrounded by tall, mossy trees full of chirping birds and wildlife. But somehow, it was impossible to speak aloud about the mad logger.

Pieced together from the many rumors running around our school, the story went something like this. Once there was a thriving logging camp back in these mountains. Business was booming one hot summer in spite of an unusual dry spell that gripped the area, and the lumber camp was projected to have its best season ever. Then one day, several lumberjacks were out cutting trees, and one of them misjudged his angle so that the tree came tumbling down on another lumberjack. One of the thick branches gave him a fearful whack on the head as it went past, and the man slumped to the ground, unconscious. A couple of the men went running back to camp to get help while two others stayed behind.

The two fellows who remained sat talking worriedly as they kept watch over their injured comrade. Suddenly, the fallen man reared up as if pulled by a string. His eyes popped open and he leapt to his feet. The lumberjacks gave shouts of surprise that turned to yells of terror when they saw the maddened gleam in the man's eyes. They were glowing with a red sort of fire as he grabbed up his fallen axe and leapt toward them, swinging fiercely, his mighty muscles gleaming in the last rays of sunlight.

When the first two lumberjacks returned with help, they stumbled across a severed hand lying in the middle of the path. At first they couldn't believe what they were seeing. But as they drew near the bloody stump, they realized that the pine needles under their feet were soaked with a sticky red liquid and that other body parts surrounded them. A large toe, a shoulder blade, a severed head with eyes popped and mouth open in a silent scream. Several men retched, and even the physician they had brought in from a nearby town was sickened. They pieced the bodies together, finally, as best they could. That's when they realized that the pieces belonged to the two loggers keeping guard—and that the injured man was gone.

They headed back to camp and told everyone what had happened. A party of men was sent out to track the mad logger, but instead they walked right into a wall of fire that sent them running for their lives. Some careless hikers had left a campfire smoldering—a dangerous thing to do in the middle of a drought—and had set the underbrush ablaze. By the time the men made it back to the camp, the whole forest was on fire behind them, and the area had to be evacuated. The wind blew something fierce that night, and the fire raged out of control. Acres burned to the ground overnight.

Before the damage could get any worse, a huge, drought-ending rainstorm blew in from the sea. The hunt for the mad logger was called off; the police and the lumberjacks agreed that he must have been killed in the fire. But a couple out joyriding in the woods a few months later claimed that a man with body aflame and wielding an axe had come running out onto the lumber road after them and had slashed several holes in their trunk. Apparently, the fellow's car still bore the marks of the axe, as well as some large scorch marks where the flaming ghost had burned the paint right off. After that, folks never went back into the burned-out woods—not on foot, and not in cars.

All this happened forty years ago or more, and though occasionally you'd still hear stories about foolish kids who went to the haunted lumber camp and never came back, Billy and I didn't believe 'em. We decided the old logging camp would be a great, creepy place to camp out. And if we could tell our friends that we saw the "ghost" . . . all the better.

It was dusk when we reached the rotting remains of a few burned-down buildings in the middle of a thicket of spruce and fir.

"This is it!" Billy said gleefully. I nodded dubiously. This place was really spooky, with strange, dark shadows surrounding the remains of the dead buildings and an air of menace oozing from the looming trees. I caught sight of a pale white shape. For a moment I took it for a severed hand and jumped backward with a gasp. Then I realized it was just a fallen branch. Billy laughed heartily, and I reluctantly joined in, pulse still pounding madly in my wrist and throat.

We put up the tent in the shelter of the tallest ruin, made a small campfire, and cooked some hot dogs and baked beans. Our merry voices were the only sounds in that dark place. I kept straining my ears to hear crickets or owls or any sort of night creatures, but the only sound I could hear was the soughing of the wind in the firs and the quiet swishing of a nearby stream. Outside the light of the fire, the night seemed very, very dark.

I hate to admit it, but I was real glad to turn in. We carefully put out the fire with stream-water, joking the whole time that we didn't want a repeat of the fire that killed the mad lumberjack. Then we crawled into the tent.

About midnight, a blaze of bright light surrounding our tent tore both Billy and me out of our sleep. I could hear the crackle of flames and the crashing sound of a tree falling nearby.

"Forest fire!" Billy shrieked, jumping up and hitting his head on the top of the tent. "Al, I thought you put the fire out!"

"I did! I did!" I shouted, struggling out of my sleeping bag.

"We've got to get out of here," Billy cried, rushing through the tent flap. I was caught in a tangle of blankets and sleeping bag and couldn't follow. Finally, I ripped the bag apart in desperation. I was crawling to the door of the tent when I heard Billy give a desperate scream that ended in a gurgle and a thump. Peering through the mosquito netting of the door, I saw the lumber camp as it once must have looked. The buildings and surrounding trees—much taller than the ones we'd seen—were all overlaid with flickering, half-seen flames. Standing in the center of it all was a tall, heavily muscled man. He was wrapped in flames, and in his hands was an axe. Lying slumped at his feet was a dark figure that I recognized at once as Billy. Only he seemed shorter than usual. That's when I realized that he had no head. My eyes popped in horror, and I scanned the ground around the flaming man until I saw Billy's severed head, face permanently frozen in a ghastly look of terror, lying a yard away from the tent flap.

I wanted to scream, but instinct kept me silent. Maybe the ghostly lumberjack hadn't seen me; maybe he didn't know I was there. I crept back into the tent as silently as I could, hoping the ghostly flames in the trees around me weren't highlighting my every move. I fumbled with the back flap, got it open, and then was running through the ghostly forest fire, running faster than I ever had in my life. *Away*, was all I could think: *I have to get away.* Around me, the flames started dying out, and I soon found myself running in total darkness. I banged right into a tree and staggered back, my eyes blazing with stars. And then I was enveloped in a huge, ghostly ball of flame. A figure towered over me, and the white dots of light in front of my eyes seemed insignificant compared to the blaze of fire crowning

THE MAD LOGGER

that massive form. I ducked frantically as an axe came swinging toward me. It swooshed just a fraction of an inch over my head. I leapt backward, dodging this way and that as the blazing figure pursued me. And then I fell over a tree stump, and my head slammed so hard against the ground that my eyes filled with tears of pain. So I never got a clear glimpse of the axe as it swung toward my neck. All I saw was flame.

8

The Sandbar

ASTORIA

I've been a fisherman all my life, and I've seen a lot of crazy things happen in these waters. But nothing had prepared me for the incident at the sandbar. It was a tragedy, and folks don't like to remember it. But somehow, now that I'm old and the days are flying past so fast I can barely count them, I feel the need to pass the story along. So the ones who died that day won't be completely lost to memory.

We pushed away from the dock in hazy, foggy weather that spring morning. The mist was already thinning in the bright sunlight overhead as my brother Jed and I set out in our boat to do some fishing in the bay. We weren't the only ones to take the notion. Many fishing boats were already on the water, and it soon became clear that the action was close to the sandbar that protected the bay. We settled in the shelter of the bar and soon were hauling in fish like there was no tomorrow. It was a record-breaking day!

Of course, what with the fishing being so good, we ignored the clouds that rolled in and kept our lines in the water. Rainy weather was nothing new in the Pacific Northwest. Jed just tossed our rain slickers out of the lockers, and we pulled them on and kept fishing.

There were about forty boats at the bar, and the wind picked up and rocked us all up and down in the increasing waves as rain started falling around us. I was used to being soaking wet out on the boat, and I calmly kept playing the fish I had hooked while water dripped off the rim of my rain hat and down my neck.

"Water's getting a mite rough," Jed observed after I'd hauled in my fish and dropped it in the cooler with the others. Jed was always a master of understatement, I thought, noticing for the first time how much the boat was rolling from side to side, from back to front. I'd been so absorbed in the sport I'd automatically compensated for the rolling of the boat without paying much attention to it.

"Looks like Tim and Eddie are packing it in," Jed added, gesturing to a couple of our buddies who'd revved up their engine and were fighting the waves as they headed back into the harbor. They were making precious little headway against the swells in the bay. 'Course, that was nothing compared to the swells out past the sandbar. The clouds were roiling overhead and the sky was so dark it might as well have been dusk rather than noontime.

The breakers from the sea were smashing into the sandbar so hard now that spray was flying everywhere, and a few had already washed right across it. Gosh almighty, it was some storm rolling our way.

"Think we should follow Eddie?" Jed asked casually, starting to reel in his line.

"Heck yeah," I said, following suit. Jed was pretty unflappable, so when he suggested heading home, I knew we were in for it.

That storm was moving in so fast that the sandbar was completely swamped by the time we got our lines in and our equipment stored. I'd pulled up the anchor and was starting the motor when Jed gave a yell of surprise that made me whip around. As my eyes took in the scene before me, my hand dropped from the engine, and it sputtered and died. Sailing through the towering ocean waves, straight across the sandbar, was a large three-masted schooner. It rose majestically against the roiling black sky, and its tattered sails whipped about in the wind and rain. The ship was glowing with blue-white fire, and you could see the heavy, rain-pocked sea right through it.

"Ghost ship!" I gasped.

"Flying Dutchman," Jed said at the same moment, and crossed himself.

The ghost ship came over the treacherous sandbar as if it didn't exist and sailed right through the first of the fishing boats. We heard the men aboard scream in terror as the blue-white hull traveled straight through them. To our horror, the fishing boat capsized in its wake. Other boats in the fleet were already gunning their engines, trying to get away from the glowing schooner as it sailed deeper into the bay.

"Get that motor running," Jed yelled frantically as a huge wave slapped over the side of our boat. "Try to keep out of its way. We've got to rescue those fellows who capsized!"

I nodded, my heart slamming in my throat. It took two tries to turn the motor over, my hands were shaking so bad, and then

THE SANDBAR

we were fighting the waves as I headed closer to the sandbar, hoping to reach the men struggling in the water.

Suddenly, Jed gave a scream of terror, and I jerked up in shock, realizing that the ghost ship was coming toward us from the starboard side. I tried to the turn the boat, and a giant wave smashed against our side, nearly capsizing us. Then my eyes and my head were filled with burning, blue-white fire that sizzled in my mind even as it chilled my wet body. As the ghost ship passed through our boat, I heard the wail of dead spirits bemoaning their fate and felt every hair on my body stand on end. I was so shocked I forgot to turn the boat into the waves, and we tipped alarmingly as the ghost ship sailed out our other side and kept going.

Jed recovered first and grabbed the wheel out of my hands, turning us enough to prevent our boat from capsizing. I was so shocked that I'd forgotten why we were heading closer to the sandbar. But Jed kept his head and shouted at me to watch for survivors in the water. I gave one last incredulous look after the ghost ship, which was slowly fading away as it sailed deeper into the harbor. Then I ran up to the bow of the ship, straining my eyes at the boiling waters and shouting out to the men in the capsized boat, hoping we'd be heard over the wind and pounding rain.

But we couldn't see anyone in the water and couldn't get too close to the massive waves slamming across the sandbar without sinking our own boat. Finally we turned back and saw that several more boats had overturned after encountering the ghost ship. We immediately joined the rest of the fishing fleet in a rescue effort. Around us, the storm abated as quickly as it had arisen, and with its passing we were able to locate and rescue several of the men who had been flung overboard when their fishing boats capsized. But many more men drowned that day, and not one body was ever recovered.

No one ever knew which of the ships lost on this stretch of the Pacific was our ghost ship. Jed still maintains that it was the infamous Flying Dutchman, but I disagree. I think it was a long-ago ship that grounded itself on the sandbar, trying to make it into the bay during a storm. I'd heard old-timers talking about such a ship, one that sometimes came sailing into the bay at the height of a storm. But that was the only time I ever saw it. Which is a mercy.

The Rivals

SISTERS

Charlene and I hated each other growing up. Really hated each other. Not strange for sisters, I guess. Sometimes you're just too close to one another to be friends. Charlene was just eleven months younger than me, and she was a big pain: always tagging along, always blaming me when she got into trouble, and always trying to one-up me.

We lived on a big ranch outside of Sisters, and we started riding horses as soon as we could walk. We began competing with each other in grade school, and that's when we really became rivals. For every ribbon I won, Charlene had to win one too. There came a time when we were equals in the saddle, but our parents refused to let us compete against one another. So we settled for competing over which competitions to enter. We argued so much about the prestige of this competition over that one that our mother threatened to make us sleep in the barn and give our room to our horses: Rebel and Sydney.

Sydney was mine—a gorgeous palomino quarter horse. Rebel, also a quarter horse, was a dashing bay with a persnickety personality that absolutely suited my persnickety little sister. We loved both horses and, oddly enough, we never fought about who had the better one. We knew they were both wonderful.

Our rivalry lasted through high school and on into college. Now we were competing in rodeos against each other, and Charlene would gloat for days if she had a faster time around the barrels than me, while I put on airs for a week if I won a calf-roping contest. Our parents sighed and put up with it. They'd had a lot of practice. But we were mellowing; at least, I was. I had decided to become a veterinarian, specializing in horse medicine, and my studies absorbed much of my time. Charlene, as a freshman, hadn't decided yet on a career and seemed more interested in boys, rodeos, and beauty pageants than schoolwork. She started competing in contests to be Rodeo Queen, and one year we even got to go to Portland to watch as she rode in the Rose Festival Parade. Mom, Dad, and I all cheered when we saw her, and I wasn't one bit jealous—which surprised me a little.

In the summer between my junior and senior year at university, Charlene and I signed up for a local rodeo competition at the end of our summer vacation, and we started training for it as soon as we got home. I'd picked a school near enough to a riding stable that I could ride every day, so I was in good shape for the competition. Charlene, on the other hand, only rode on weekends when she was at school, and she wasn't ready at all. I thought about pointing this out to her; in fact, once upon a time I would have jeered at her until she burst into tears and ran to her room. But I found that I no longer wanted to hurt my little sister. She, however, irked by my "mature old lady" attitude, finally bet me her brand-new blue dress that she would win the competition. Well, that did it. I'd been drooling over that dress, and Charlene knew it. I got even more serious about

THE RIVALS

my training, fitting in two sessions a day around my summer job at the veterinary clinic.

Then Charlene got a call just six weeks before the competition. Her best friend Jeannie was going to Paris for ten days and wanted Charlene to go along. That was a tough one for Charlene. She still wasn't quite ready for the upcoming rodeo, but she knew that a free trip to Paris doesn't come along every day. So she went, figuring that she'd still have four weeks to train before the competition.

I was surprised at how much I missed my little sister. We'd had a few in-depth conversations this summer, which had completely flummoxed our dad, and had even done some double dating. Mom took the whole thing in stride. She'd hated *her* little sister growing up, and now they were best friends. So she totally got it.

I went to bed early the night Charlene was due to fly home from Paris. I'd gotten a migraine working at the animal clinic, and my head was pounding and I was seeing silvery spots before my eyes by quitting time. The veterinarian had to call my folks because I was too sick to drive myself home. They put me to bed and pulled the shades, and I hunched down and tried to sleep through the dull pounding. It seemed to take forever to drift off.

I was awakened when someone shook my shoulder. "Go 'way. I'm tryin' to sleep," I mumbled into my pillow.

"Get up, Judy! I need to talk to you," Charlene's voice said in my ear. I frowned a bit and rolled over. I hadn't expected to see Charlene until sometime tomorrow afternoon, when her friend's parents dropped her off.

"You're home early," I said, rubbing hard at my eyes to get the sleep out of them. Charlene hadn't bothered to turn on the light. Or had she? There was a kind of glow around her that made me think that someone had left a night-light on in the bathroom across the hall.

"Yeah," she said, sitting down on the bed. "Much earlier than I'd planned."

I propped myself up against the pillows and looked at Charlene. Her red hair was in two long braids, and she wore a dark beret on her head as if she were a French student.

"Nice hat," I said, to tease her.

"I got it in Paris. Don't you think it makes me look like an artist?" my little sister said, turning her head this way and that so I could admire it.

"Definitely," I replied, stretching out the kinks in my shoulders. To my relief, my headache was gone.

"Listen, Judy. I don't have much time," Charlene said, suddenly serious. "I wanted to talk to you . . . *needed* to talk to you. So I came back."

Her words made my skin prickle. I'd never heard such a tone from her before. And what did she mean when she said she came back? Of course she came back. She lived here.

"What did you want to talk about?" I asked, setting aside her strange words for the present.

"The rodeo. The blue dress. You and me," Charlene said.

I digested this for a moment. "What about you and me?" I asked.

"Well, I guess I wanted to say I'm sorry I've been such a pest, and that I kept getting you in trouble when we were growing up. I really admired you, and I wanted to be just like you. Only you never had time for me unless we were fighting. At least, that's what I thought then. Anyway, I'm sorry we wasted so much time fighting when we could have been friends, like we've been this summer."

I felt tears prick my eyes. "Me too," I said. "I'm sorry too."

"I want you to have my blue dress," Charlene continued. "And I want you to ride in that rodeo and win it. Win it for me!"

"We'll both ride in the rodeo," I said firmly. "And it won't matter which of us wins. And afterward I want you to wear the blue dress when we go out to celebrate."

Charlene smiled. It was a sad, wistful smile.

"I want you to have the blue dress," she said again. "And always remember that I love you. Tell Mom and Dad I love them too."

And she disappeared.

My jaw dropped in astonishment. Where did she go? "Charlene!" I called. And then louder: "Charlene! Charlene!"

I groped for the light, and as I snapped it on my Mom came into the room. "Charlene's not home yet, Judy," she told me.

"She's spending the night at the airport hotel with the Parkers, remember? How are you feeling, honey?"

I stared up at my mother and started to shake all over. "But she was just here," I protested, my heart hammering against my chest. "I just saw her here!"

"You must have been dreaming," Mom said, sitting down in the exact same place where Charlene had sat a moment before. "Not surprising with that migraine you had. Go back to sleep."

Maybe she was right, I thought. Maybe it was a dream. But I was filled with a sense of dread so strong it roiled my stomach and made me want to vomit. I didn't fall back asleep until dawn.

I was awakened for the second time by the sound of muffled voices from the lower hallway. Then I heard my Mom cry out: "No! Please, God, no!"

I shot out of bed and down the hall without bothering with a robe. My nightgown flapped around my legs as I ran down the stairs. I stopped three steps from the bottom when I saw the policeman standing in the doorway, and my Mom crouched on the floor, hugging herself tightly as if cushioning a terrible blow to her abdomen. Dad was ashen, leaning against the doorframe, unable to move.

"Mommy? Daddy?" I whispered, as if I were a child of five rather than a grown-up college student. They didn't move. Neither of them could speak. I stared at the police officer and said in a high-pitched tone: "Charlene?"

The officer nodded and quietly told me what he had told my parents. The plane Charlene and the Parkers were on had crashed into the sea during the night. There were no survivors.

I sat down on the steps and watched the officer nod to my too-still parents and quietly leave, closing the front door behind him. I don't think they noticed.

The next couple of weeks were awful. There was no body to bury, so we had a memorial service for Charlene. Her horse, Rebel, kept looking and looking for her every time I entered the stable, so I spent a lot of time currying and brushing him, until my own horse Sydney became jealous. I felt so dark and dull inside, and the pain was so intense that I sometimes had to crouch down like my Mom and rock back and forth until it eased a little. I told my parents about my meeting with Charlene, the night she died. I gave them her message, and I think it helped a little. I know it helped me.

My parents sat in the front row the day of the rodeo. Tears were streaming down my mother's face during the whole competition. I won it with ease, urged on by the sight of my Mom and Dad waving the blue dress. I won it for Charlene. And when the judges shook my hand at the end of the rodeo, I thought I heard Charlene say softly, from somewhere far off and yet quite close to my ear: "Good job, Judy."

10

Cold

ASHLAND

It was one of those stifling hot days you get in early September. My buddy Lisa and I had retreated to her room in the basement of the Suzanne Homes dorm to study, since it was cooler down there than anywhere else in building. We were both in our sophomore year at SOU—that's Southern Oregon University—and were beginning to realize that our teachers had been taking it easy on us last year. Our classwork was already at a nightmarish level and was bound to get worse before it got better—if it ever got better.

We studied late into the evening until my head was swimming with more facts than I could handle. *Dang it, I should just drop out of school and get a job flipping burgers*, I thought grumpily. I slammed my book shut and stretched. "I'd better get back to my room," I said to Lisa, reluctance plain in my voice. I lived at the top of the dorm, and the rooms up there were too hot for my comfort.

"You can stay here for the night if you want," Lisa said, turning away from her desk to look at me. "Sarah's gone home for the weekend." Sarah was her roommate this semester.

I felt my face light up with relief. "Great, thanks! I'll just run up and get my jammies!"

I was back in two ticks, thankful to be out of my stuffy room, and soon had settled into Sarah's empty bed, reveling in the relative coolness of the basement. "Thanks, Lisa," I said, as she turned out the light by her own bed, plunging the room into darkness.

"No problem," Lisa replied as she settled down under the sheets to sleep.

I was awakened around midnight when a cool breeze swept through the room. It cut right through the light sheets of my borrowed bed and sent a deep chill through my entire body. I shivered uncontrollably, and my teeth began chattering. It was cold. Horribly cold.

I sat up and groped desperately for the blanket I'd tossed on the floor earlier that evening. That's when I heard a soft tap-tap-tap sound at the door. I blinked, narrowing my eyes against the grayness of the dorm room until I could make out the faint outline of the door. The sound came again—a soft, timid tapping. Across the room, Lisa sat up groggily and said: "Ugh! It's freezing in here. And what's that sound?"

"Someone's at the door," I answered, my teeth chattering with cold.

"Jeez!" Lisa said. "Honestly, it's too early in the sem . . . semester . . . " she paused, trying to control the chattering of her own teeth as the room temperature dropped still further. She tried again: "It's too early in the semester to pull an all-nighter!"

She stumbled out of bed, knocked her shin against her desk chair, and cursed. I made it out of bed with a bit more grace, hopping as the icy-cold floor stung my bare feet.

Tap-tap-tap. The timid knock came a third time, and this time I answered it while Lisa grumbled and groped about in the dark for her bathrobe.

I swung the door open and almost fell over in the blast of frigid air that struck my face. My hair actually blew straight up, as if a wind were hitting it from a fan on the floor. In front of me, shivering in the dull light cast by the hall lights, stood a small boy. He was soaking wet from head to toe. Water was dripping down onto the floor of the hallway and puddling about his feet.

I gaped at the little boy. How'd he get here? Why was he all wet? Behind me, Lisa came to the door, shaking with cold. She took one look at the little boy and fell to her knees in sympathy. "Sweetie, what's wrong?" she crooned.

"I'm c . . . c . . . cold," the little boy wailed.

"Get him a towel," Lisa said to me, and I ran back into the room to fetch a towel from the rack. But the rack was bare.

"Lisa, I can't find one," I called out.

"Stay right there, sweetie," Lisa said to the little boy and came hurrying into the room to help me search. I stumbled over the blanket I'd dropped on the floor when I'd gotten into bed. Grabbing it, I rushed toward the lighted doorway and the dripping-wet child.

Before my eyes, the little boy suddenly shattered into a million little floating specks of white light. I skidded to a halt, blanket-wrapped arms still outstretched, and shrieked. The light-specks whirled strangely, as if they were caught in a mini-tornado, and a chilly breeze swept up from the floor and whipped around my legs and arms, blowing my hair straight up once again. Then the lights were gone, leaving behind only a puddle of water in the doorway.

"Oh, my Lord!" Lisa whimpered from my left. She held a large beach towel clasped to her chest. She dropped the towel and started wringing her hands. My legs were shaking so much

COLD

that I collapsed onto the freezing-cold floor. My heart was thumping so fast I thought I was having a heart attack.

Gradually, the room around us heated up to its normal temperature, and the terror caused by the dripping boy's appearance slowly slipped away.

Lisa staggered over to her bed and sank onto the mattress. She buried her face in her hands for a long moment, then she looked up at me in the light slanting in through the door. "Did that just happen?" she asked quietly, her voice high and squeaky with shock. "Or did I dream it?"

"It happened," I assured her, twisting the edge of the blanket around and around with shaking hands. "We both couldn't have had the exact same dream."

"I'd heard this place was haunted, but I never believed it," Lisa said. She slowly rose and got two bottles of water from the small refrigerator she kept by her desk. She handed me one and drank deeply from the other.

I'd never heard any rumors of a haunting in this dorm and questioned her about it. Lisa sat back down on the bed and told me what she had heard. It was said that a man-made lake stood underneath the campus and that the Suzanne Homes building had been constructed on top of it. One day, shortly before the basement was finished, a little boy decided to play in the lake. He dragged a mattress downstairs and tried to float on it like a boat. But it sank, and the little boy drowned in the icy-cold water. Ever since then, students have claimed that the ghost of a little boy wanders in and out of the rooms in the basement of Suzanne Homes.

"I thought the stories were complete rot," Lisa said. "Until now."

I shivered again, and stared at the slowly drying puddle of water in the doorway. "That poor kid," I whispered. I was still frightened by the strange experience, but I felt sad too.

"Yeah," said Lisa. "Poor kid."

She got up and firmly shut the door of her room. "I don't know about you, but I won't be answering any more nighttime knockings," she said, shrugging out of her bathrobe and getting back into bed.

"Me neither," I said, crawling back into my own borrowed bed. I spent a long time that night staring at the gray shadows on the ceiling, torn by fear of the supernatural and sorrow for a cold, little boy. And I was suddenly glad that my dorm room was on the top floor.

Turning over on my side, I slept at last, and when I woke in the morning, the puddle was gone.

11

The Cabin

MOUNT HOOD

I caught a glimpse of some deer grazing a few yards off the hiking trail on the north slope of Mount Hood and immediately snuck into the brush with my camera, determined to get some close-ups. It looked like one of them had a little fawn, always a fun picture if you can get it.

I have no idea how I got lost. One minute I was blissfully snapping away with my digital camera and the next I was stumbling and cursing my way over fallen trees, through dense forest, and alongside at least one set of brambles that left me scraped and irritable. Occasionally I glimpsed the tall, snow-covered peak of the mountain through gaps in the trees, but at the moment the sight was an irritation rather than a delight. I wanted to hike up to my favorite lookout and take pictures of that peak, not slog along through a forest without even a deer trail to guide me.

After about an hour of wandering through the dense woods, I came to a small canyon. By this time, the clouds had blotted out the sun, the wind had picked up, and a heavy rain was falling. Just great. Talk about adding insult to injury. I tucked my camera under my shirt and turned into the canyon, which would at least

THE CABIN

provide shelter of a sort from the wind. I wandered miserably along the gulch, hoping to find an overhang or cave of some sort in which to shelter from the blasted rain.

To my surprise, I soon spotted a rotting log cabin with its roof partially caved in. *What was that doing here,* I wondered. But I wasn't going to question my good fortune. Here was shelter from the rain, and I was going to take advantage of it.

As I approached the decrepit cabin, the temperature in the air plummeted several degrees. I shivered in surprise. A few moments before it had been a balmy, if very wet, summer day. But now it felt like late autumn. I clutched my camera more tightly under my shirt and ran across the little glade and through the rotting doorway of the cabin. The beating of the rain ceased abruptly, but the cold increased. My teeth started to chatter as I looked around the one-room cabin. On the left side was a mass of mossy debris where the roof had fallen in. On the right side was a pot-bellied stove, rusted to pieces. Immediately to my left was a very old rotting rectangular shape that must once have been a mattress.

It was a dark, creepy place. I shivered, feeling strangely like a trespasser, and had a strong impulse to flee back into the rainstorm. I pulled out my camera, hoping that taking some photos would calm my nerves, and snapped a few shots of the old mattress, the fallen ceiling, and the rotting stove. But instead of feeling better, I felt worse. Like someone was standing directly behind me, waiting to pounce. I whirled around, but there was nothing there. Defiantly, I snapped a picture of the open doorway. And then a voice roared: "Go away!" The ghastly overtones brought more of the roof down in a shower of splinters and mud and moss.

My heart leapt right into my mouth. I had to swallow several times before I could release the shriek that was stuck in my throat. Then I ran as fast as my legs would carry me, out of the house, down the small canyon, through the tall trees and underbrush. I hurtled over fallen logs like an Olympic champion, slipping and sliding on mud and fallen pine needles, running straight through dense brush. I even forded a stream, not bothering to look for a bridge or a fallen tree to ease my passage. The rain poured down onto me, soaking my hair, my clothes, and my shoes. And still I made my way down, down, down the mountain, until I finally, thankfully, stumbled across a road.

And low and behold, I knew that road. It was the same one I'd traveled on to get here, and my car was parked only a few yards away. Somehow I stumbled, shivering and exhausted, into my SUV and drove to the nearest inn I could find. I *really* needed a drink! I was covered in mud and pine needles, and I brushed ineffectually at my clothes and tried to wipe my face clean on a napkin I found in the car. Then I went into the tavern. I knew I was still a sight, but I didn't care.

My hair was dripping uncomfortably down my neck, and my hands were still shaking as I sipped a beer and tried to calm down. Guess the guy next to me at the bar thought I needed cheering up. He started talking casually about the weather and the local sports teams, and gradually I calmed down and was able to respond. Finally he said: "You look a little shook up, my lad. Want to talk about it?"

I didn't really. It seemed so strange. But after all, no one here knew me, so what could it hurt? I told them about finding the narrow canyon and the abandoned cabin within it. I even mentioned the feeling of being watched, and the unusual coldness.

As I spoke, the bartender came down from the far end of the bar to listen, and the fellows around us fell silent.

"I think that cabin is haunted," I concluded, failing to mention the invisible voice. I didn't want them to think I was completely crazy.

"Well, well. I think you may have stumbled upon Hermit Pickett's old cabin," the man next to me said when I concluded my tale. "I don't suppose you could find your way back there, by any chance?"

I shook my head. "I was completely lost, both before and afterward," I said ruefully. "Why? Who was Hermit Pickett?"

In the end, everyone in the bar contributed something to the story, stumbling over each other in their eagerness. It seemed that Hermit Pickett was an old-time placer miner turned bank robber who stole a fortune in money and gold from a Wells Fargo wagon and fled from Idaho to Mount Hood with his loot. Fortunately for him—or perhaps unfortunately—the police nabbed the wrong fellow for the crime, and Pickett got away home free. Still, for some reason, he headed into the mountains with his ill-gotten gains, built himself a log cabin, and lived the life of a hermit for many years. Eventually, however, guilt overcame him, and he went back to Idaho to confess to the crime and free the other bloke from prison. Pickett was already in ill health, and he died a few hours after his confession. The police tried to follow his directions back to the cabin, where he'd stashed the gold and money, but they couldn't find it. According to local legend, the treasure is still buried underneath the hermit's cabin, somewhere on Mount Hood.

"Don't suppose you saw any gold bars while you were there?" my new friend asked wistfully. I shook my head and shivered a little, remembering the creepy feeling I'd had in the log cabin, and the voice that told me to go away.

"No gold," I said, tossing money onto the bar and getting to my feet. "Just a ghost."

I left the tavern in a thoughtful mood. What I had told the other men was true. There was no way I could retrace my steps to the log cabin. And there was no way I wanted to, treasure or no treasure. That ghostly voice had been too much for me.

When I got home that night, I loaded the digital pictures onto my computer and then fell into bed. So it wasn't until the next morning that I saw the picture of the darkly glowing, yellow-eyed figure floating in the log cabin doorway, right in the place where I'd heard the invisible voice. I screamed when the picture flipped up on my computer screen and made a run for the next room, heart hammering painfully against my ribs. Finally, I regained my composure and went back to the computer. The figure was still there, looking more like a darkly glowing column than a person. For a moment, my shaking hand hovered over the delete key. But I stopped myself. After all, how many people had a picture of a real ghost?

The more I thought back on my encounter in the cabin, the more convinced I was that I'd done the right thing by running away. I was lucky the ghost let me off with a verbal warning. Who knows what would have happened had I tried to stay and search for his treasure?

12

The Golden Hand

MEDFORD

He never paid much attention to the neighbors living on his city block until the day the pretty middle-aged widow moved in two doors down from him. She was plump and dark with sparkling eyes, and she always wore black gloves on her hands, even indoors. He went out of his way to meet her, and they often "bumped" into each other in the street and stood talking.

One day, as the widow flirtatiously brushed the hair back from her forehead, he caught a glimpse of gold under the glove on her right hand. When he asked her about it, she grinned coquettishly and told him that she had lost a hand a few years back and now wore a golden hand in its place. In that moment, a terrible lust woke in his heart—not to possess the lady herself, but to possess the solid gold arm that she wore under her long black gloves.

He courted the widow with every stratagem known to him: flowers, trips to the theater, gifts, and compliments. At first, she remained aloof. But he continued to pursue her with ardor, taking her to the best restaurants, singing love songs outside her window, and buying her the expensive chocolates she favored. And finally, he won her heart. Within a month, they were standing in front of a minister, promising to love one another until death. And within another month, he was a widower and had buried his poor wife in the local cemetery—without her golden hand. It had been so easy. A slow poison, administered daily, so that its affects resembled a wasting disease. No one—not his wife, not the family doctor, not their neighbors—suspected murder. And the night after the funeral, he slept with the golden hand under his pillow.

It was a dark night. Clouds covered the moon, and the wind came whistling down the chimney and rattled the shutters of the townhouse. Outside his window, a blue light bobbed for a moment, and the faintest whisper of a voice murmured: "Where's my golden hand?" The man stirred nervously against his pillow but didn't wake, and slowly the blue light faded and disappeared.

A few moments later, the front door opened with its normal creak and groan, and footsteps sounded in the lower hall. A voice called out: "Where's my hand? My golden hand?" The man jerked awake and looked wildly around the dark room. No one was there, and the sound in the lower hall ceased the moment he opened his eyes.

Deciding he was having a dream, the man turned over and went back to sleep. As soon as his eyes closed, the phantom footsteps sounded again, walking slowly and deliberately toward the stairs leading to the second floor. A cold breeze swirled through the upper hallway and underneath the door. The man's eyes popped open. For a moment, he thought he heard footsteps on the stairs, and a voice groaned: "Where's my golden hand?" The man sat bolt upright in bed, his body shaking. Then the wind died down, and all was silent. Nervously, he got out of bed and bolted the bedroom door. "It was just the breeze," he told

THE GOLDEN HAND

himself bracingly as he slipped back under the covers. But he didn't believe it, and his body trembled underneath the heavy quilts and did not grow warm.

For a long time the man lay awake, listening sharply for a sound—any sound. And all the time he thought about his dead wife. Once he turned over and felt under his pillow for the golden hand. It was still there. And his wife, he knew, lay buried in the cemetery.

"This is nonsense!" he muttered at last, and turned over to sleep.

He had just dozed off when the door to his room slammed open with a bang and a wild wind whipped around the room, scattering papers and books and clothing and table coverings every which way. He shot awake with a terrified shriek and sat up, startled by the sudden noise. His heart hammered so hard and fast it pained him, and adrenaline raced through his body. Then he froze in horror as blue-white light materialized before him and bobbed toward the bed. Before his eyes, the light slowly grew larger, taking on the shape of his dead wife. "Where's my golden hand?" she moaned, her dark eyes blazing with red fire. "Give me my golden hand!"

He tried to speak, but his mouth was so dry with fear that he could only make soft gasping noises. The glowing phantom moved closer to him, her once-lovely face twisted into a hideous green mask. "You stole my life and you stole my hand. Give me back my golden hand!" the dead wife howled. The noise rose higher and higher, and the phantom pulsed with a blue light that smote his eyes, making them water.

He cowered back against his pillows, and the hard shape of the golden hand pressed against his back. And then he felt the golden hand twitch underneath him as the mangled blue-white phantom that had been his wife swooped down upon him, pressing his face against the pillow in a suffocating blue cloud. He tried to scream, but his voice was cut off suddenly by a terrible pressure against his throat. The world went black.

The next morning, when the housemaid came into the room with her master's morning cup of tea, she found him lying dead on the floor, with the golden hand clenched tightly around his throat.

13

Underground

PENDLETON

We'd timed our visit to Oregon to coincide with the Pendleton Round-Up and had managed to snag one of the very last hotel rooms in town. My husband, a big rodeo fan, was as excited as a little kid to be attending the famous Pendleton Round-Up. Myself, I was eagerly anticipating a tour of the famous—or should I say infamous?—Pendleton Underground.

According to the literature I'd read prior to the visit, Pendleton was a small village first settled in the 1860s or thereabouts by a fellow named Goodwin. It was mostly a farming community that didn't begin to boom until prospectors found gold in the Blue Mountains. After this discovery, Pendleton became a stop for supply wagons, as well as an entertainment capital where miners could spend their hard-won gold and where cowboys and ranchers could come to drink, gamble in the thirty-two saloons, and visit one of the eighteen bordellos.

Chinese workers came in abundance to work in the mines or do business in town. They were not always welcomed by the general populace, so they burrowed underground and began digging tunnels from business to business, cellar to cellar, living and working in the tunnels they had dug. It was estimated that Pendleton's labyrinth of underground tunnels, dug by the Chinese between 1870 and 1930, wound for more than seventy miles beneath the town. Through the years, the Pendleton underground tunnels and rooms were used by Chinese workers, Prohibitionists, opium addicts, ice-cream stores, butcher shops, speakeasies, saloons, card parlors, and even a bowling alley!

Rumors abounded about the Underground. One story claimed that a pair of train robbers who used the tunnels to store their ill-gotten goods had died in the dark passages under an old house during a gun battle over the stolen gold. It was said that the ghosts of the robbers still haunted the place, and people could sometimes hear them crying, "It's my gold!"

I shivered in delight as I recounted the legend to my husband. Being pragmatic, he just laughed. But he did agree to accompany me on the tour of the Pendleton Underground.

I picked up the phone at once and booked the very next tour. My husband laughed as I bounced on my toes in excitement and danced around the hotel room, as giddy as a child. I was acting even sillier than he had on the first night of the roundup!

After a quick lunch, we went to the tour headquarters and gathered with a large group of people, all interested in the story of the mysterious tunnels beneath our feet. I told my husband that we were probably standing over a tunnel right now. The tour guide heard me and confirmed that part of the Pendleton Underground was directly below us. I grinned in triumph.

We watched a brief film, and then we were escorted outside. We walked around a corner and stopped so the tour guide could tell us a short story about the cowboys who had stood on that very spot and called up to the working girls in the rooms above our heads. I craned my neck upward, trying to picture the scene. Above me, something scarlet flickered in and out of view at the corner of my eye. I blinked and rocked back on my heels, chills running down my spine. For a moment, I'd stared into bold black eyes over a gaudily painted red mouth. The flash of scarlet had been dyed feathers framing an attractive heart-shaped face.

I stared openmouthed at the empty window above me until I was jostled by the moving crowd around me. Everyone else was walking down the steps beside me.

The skin between my shoulder blades pricked with apprehension as I blindly followed my husband down the staircase. What had just happened? Had I imagined the face in the window?

We went through a door and found ourselves in a cellar that once housed a saloon. I shivered as the temperature around me dropped more than ten degrees. It was cold in here. I wished vainly for my sweater, left back in the hotel room, as I stared at the re-created Old West scene. Cowboy mannequins lounged around tables and played cards, while our tour guide stood behind the polished bar and discussed the role of the saloon in the days of the gold rush. My husband was absolutely fascinated.

I listened with half an ear as I poked around the basement room and looked at the exhibits, trying to imagine what it was like to drink and play cards underground, a lump of gold in my pocket and a gun at my side. The tour guide beckoned us onward, and I trotted obediently behind my husband, who was chatting eagerly with a rodeo enthusiast.

When we entered a re-created Chinese laundry, I was hit with a wave of not-quite-nausea. I swayed as my eyes swam with strange, out-of-focus colors. My stomach flip-flopped strangely, my spine went rigid, and the skin on my shoulders and arms prickled with goose bumps. For a moment, I could hear water swishing, and, beside me, a man's voice said something in Chinese. I gasped and whirled, but no one was there.

As suddenly as it had come, the nausea faded and my head was clear again. The room swam back into focus, and I realized that the rest of the tour had moved next door into the re-created ice-cream shop. I followed hurriedly.

Spooked by my experience, I stayed by his side as the tour guide discussed the use of this space for ice-cream storage and then took us through a doorway into a long underground room full of small cots and benches. The room was lined with windows that looked out onto a tunnel-hallway lit by glassed-in openings in the sidewalk above.

The guide stepped into the room, which housed a demonstration of the famous Pendleton wool industry, and spoke knowledgeably about the exhibit. A loud buzzing like the noise of a large drill prevented me from hearing much of the talk. Some workmen must be fixing an exhibit, I supposed. I glanced around in annoyance and whispered to my husband, "I wish they'd stop drilling." He blinked in surprise and whispered back, "What drilling?" That's when I realized the buzzing sound was only in my head.

I shrugged, and my husband turned his attention back to the lecturing tour guide. Around me, the buzzing sound grew louder and became a flood of words and phrases in broken English and Chinese. My stomach turned over as strange bits of color flashed first here and then there in the room. For a brief moment, I saw an almost-invisible Chinese man doing calculations on an abacus made of some kind of black wood.

UNDERGROUND

The hands—the only clearly visible part of the man—were rapidly moving red beads back and forth on little wooden bars.

"Come on, Sally. Don't lag behind," my husband said impatiently, pulling at my hand. Instantly, my vision cleared and I was back in the present. I staggered and clutched the wall for a moment. Then I followed my husband through the door and into the tunnel itself, which was constructed of dark basalt stones, smoothed fairly flat on the outside and carefully mortared together. I could see through the large windows right back into the room where we had just been standing. I glanced toward the place where I had seen the hands holding the abacus, shuddered once, and resolutely kept my eyes forward as we navigated around a corner and into the next area.

We passed through a place where a thriving butcher's shop had conducted its business. I blinked cautiously as I looked around the room, but everything stayed in focus, for which I was grateful. It was fascinating to see the old posters advertising low prices for meat, the old-style cash register, and the cold room where the meat was kept. I was feeling much more myself now, having thrust aside the odd occurrences to think about when we were aboveground.

Then I stepped into the next room, an old card room that had been used as a bar during Prohibition, and heard an alarm bell jangling desperately from somewhere overhead. In front of me was the re-created scene of a card party, with rough-looking fellows sitting around a table, eyeing one another suspiciously. Above the mannequins, the little bell was still vibrating, as if the string that activated it had just been pulled. No one else seemed to notice the vibrating bell or the sound of feet thudding rapidly. I tensed, wanting to run away with the fleeing feet.

My husband noticed my distress and whispered, "Are you all right?" I nodded slightly, unable to speak, and gratefully followed the rest of the tour down another tunnel and into a brighter room once used as a bowling alley. Then we were back on the street in the fresh air, and I was panting with combined fear and exhaustion. What was happening? Was I losing my mind?

My husband was very concerned. "You look ill, honey," he said. "Do you want to go back to the hotel? We can take the rest of the tour another day."

"I'm fine," I snapped. How could I explain to my pragmatic husband that I was seeing things in the tunnels? He'd put it down to tiredness or say I was coming down with something.

The tour headed down the street toward the old bordello, which was the next stop. I followed determinedly, so my husband went with me. Taking hold of my hand, he eyed me sideways once in a while to make sure I was all right.

We climbed the "steps to heaven" and toured the rooms of the old bordello without any distressing color flashes or visions on my part, though I thought my husband's eyes would fall out when he saw some of the decorations on the walls. Then we were at street level again, watching our guide open the locked door leading to our last stop on the Underground tour. I started to shake at the thought of going back underground. We were going to see a Chinese jail just below our feet. Apparently the Chinese policed their own in the early days. I drew in a deep breath and followed my husband downstairs into a musty room filled with bunk beds and tables and a cooking stove. There were Buddhas and Chinese hats on the top shelf by the stove.

A gong hung next to me, and as I looked at it, the not-quite-nausea swept over me and the tour guide's voice faded away. I stared at the gong in a cowardly manner, listening to several male voices conversing leisurely in Mandarin Chinese behind me. I heard someone laugh—a merry sound—and finally turned to gaze at a jolly man cooking something over a stove that looked similar to the one in the re-creation. Behind him, a group of men sat around a table playing mah-jongg, and another man lit incense before a little altar in the corner. It was all so clear that for a moment I thought I could walk right up to the table and join the game.

From somewhere far away, I heard my husband's voice urging me along. I walked forward slowly, nodding to the men at the mah-jongg table. They beamed and nodded back, not at all surprised to see me. I risked a quick glance down and saw that I was wearing a dress and held a basket on my arm. I wondered who I was, back in this time.

I walked with my basket into a small side room once used as an opium den and set my basket down beside a man lounging languidly on the bed, smoking deeply from his pipe. He dreamily nodded his thanks to me, and my lips moved, speaking to him in Chinese, a language I did not know.

Suddenly, the brightness died from the scene. The bed was empty; the room was faded and musty. I stared in shock at the old platform where opium users had once smoked their pipes, willing myself back in time for just one moment more. Then my husband's hands closed on my shoulders, and he turned me to face him. His eyes were wide with worry, and I could feel his hands trembling against my shoulders. "Sally, what's wrong? You looked like you were in a trance."

"I . . . I think I should get out of here," I gasped, swaying slightly with vertigo. Coming back to the present day was a shock to my overwrought nervous system. My husband took my arm and half carried me out of the tunnels and up to the daylight world. I stood trembling for a long moment, gasping in the fresh air.

"Pretty creepy down there," my husband remarked, watching me closely. He didn't believe in the supernatural, but even he could tell something had happened to me. "You can tell me all about it when we get back to the hotel."

I nodded gratefully. I needed time to think about what I'd seen before I discussed it with anyone.

My husband guided me to the tour headquarters, where we thanked our guide and bought a souvenir book before heading into the sunlit street. As we walked back toward the car, I looked down at one of the purple-glass windows in the sidewalk that helped light the tunnels below. In my mind, I saw a pair of hands busy with an abacus and a man smoking a pipe full of opium. I'd never thought of myself as psychic, but I was convinced that I had truly walked into the past during my time in the tunnels below Pendleton. Glancing up at my pragmatic husband, I wasn't sure how much I should tell him. Would he believe me? I wasn't sure I believed it myself, and it had happened to me!

"What's next on the roundup schedule?" I asked, watching my husband's face light up as he grabbed the battered schedule from his pocket. Gesturing animatedly, he spread the paper on the hood of our car and started enumerating the possibilities. I leaned next to him and glanced through the information on the sheet, happy to put the ghosts of the past behind me and look to the future—which had better, I informed my eager spouse, involve some ice cream.

14

Is It Rue?

HECETA HEAD

It's a fairly steep climb up the cliff to the Heceta Head lighthouse, but the view is worth it. I like to jog along the beach and then up to the light as part of my weekend workout. I slowed, as I always do, when I neared the old lighthouse keeper's house. These days it's a bed-and-breakfast, but originally it was the home of the caretakers who looked after the light. It's a beauty of a house that still looks much the same today as when it was first raised, or so my daddy told me. But I wouldn't stay there. Not for any money.

They say the old lighthouse keeper's house is haunted, and I confess to feeling a few skin prickles as I got closer to the keeper's place. I glanced up at the top window, wondering if I might see a gray figure standing there, but it was empty. I sighed in relief and picked up speed, jogging up toward the spectacular view from the lighthouse.

Heceta Head lighthouse is in the Devil's Elbow, and the waters hereabouts can be treacherous to boats at night. Ships' captains claimed they could see the light from twenty miles out at sea, and it has saved many lives through the years. But the life of an old-time lighthouse keeper—before automation came—was

IS IT RUE?

no picnic. Tending the light was a round-the-clock job, what with keeping the oil lamp lit at night and cleaning 640 prisms in the eight-paneled lens. All this work kept passing ships from crashing on the rocks lining the coast. Lighthouse keepers also tended to live in isolated places, which was probably hard on their families.

I paused, panting, by the fence and stared out at the view. Waves crashed far below me, and the sea was endless. I drew in a deep breath of salty air, glad to be alive. Looking down from atop that dangerous cliff reminded me once again of the ghost in the keeper's house. Somewhere along the line, folks started calling her Rue, though there aren't any records to tell us if that was really her name. In fact, no one knows exactly who the Heceta Head ghost really is. The story that follows is the one repeated most.

Back in the late 1890s, a new lighthouse keeper came to Heceta Head with his wife and their small daughter. While the keeper was busy working, his wife tended the house and looked after the little toddler. Things were going well for the couple until the day their child was killed in an accident. No one knows, after all this time, exactly what happened. Some folks swear the toddler pitched herself over the cliff, while others claim the baby drowned. But everyone agrees that the poor woman was devastated by the loss of her little one. When she died, her spirit stayed in the house where her baby once lived.

My family first became aware of the story back in the 1970s, when my daddy was serving at a local restaurant on the weekends to put himself through college. He met the new caretaker one afternoon, and the two of them really hit it off. The caretaker was full of stories about the crazy house he'd moved into with his wife. It was full of funny creaks and groans.

"It sounds as if someone is climbing the steps from the cellar," he said, waving his hand for emphasis. "I opened the door, thinking it was my wife needing a hand, but no one was there. Other times, the dishes rattle in the cupboard so bad you'd think we were having an earthquake. And there's this clicking sound, as if someone were switching the lights off and on. Drives me crazy. My wife says it's just the wind shaking the house, but I don't know. It gives me goose bumps."

The caretaker brought his wife in for lunch a few weeks later, and she had another story to tell. "Things keep moving around the house," she said. "I'll be doing chores, and I'll put something down for a moment to answer the phone, and it disappears. After tearing the house apart, I'll find it put back in the closet or drawer or cupboard where it belongs. I think my husband is tidying up after me," she added with an affectionate grin.

"I keep telling her I'm not," he protested. "Really. Tell him about the silk stocking."

"Do I want to know about the silk stocking?" my daddy asked, faintly alarmed.

"We put rat poison up in the attic," the wife said. "We kept hearing noises up there at night. When we checked it the next day, the poison had vanished, and in its place was an old-fashioned woman's silk stocking!"

"That's odd. It sounds like you've got a ghost in the house," my daddy joked.

The couple looked at him strangely, and he realized they'd both gone pale. He mumbled an apology and rushed to refill their water glasses. When he got back, the wife asked him to sit with them for a moment since they were the only customers in the room at the time.

"We do have a ghost," she said. "My husband has seen her. He ran upstairs once to get his keys and saw a gray figure in a long skirt crossing the hallway. She vanished through a closed door into a guest bedroom we never use."

"Gave me the creeps," the caretaker said with a shiver. He took his wife's hand with trembling fingers. "Tell him about the card party."

"We were playing cards with friends one night," the wife related, "and suddenly a high-pitched voice screamed from the middle of the room. Even our cats jumped at the sound. No one else was there. It was . . . freaky. Now you tell him about the carpenter." The husband nodded soberly and motioned my daddy closer as he started to relate the tale.

A workman was hired by the Forest Service to make repairs to the keeper's house shortly after the couple moved in. The poor fellow had a string of bad luck from the get-go. Tools and sandpaper vanished into thin air, only to reappear in the most unlikely spot imaginable. Locks wouldn't stay locked. Things came to a head one bright, sunny morning when the carpenter decided to take care of a few items in the attic. The attic was only accessible through a trapdoor in the upstairs hallway. The ceilings were tall, so the carpenter had to climb to the top of a stepladder and then stretch up as far as he could to grasp the attic floor and haul himself up.

On this particular day, the carpenter was polishing the glass of the attic window. He caught a glimpse of a moving figure behind him and turned around. He found himself face to face with a woman in a long flowing dress. She had the slim figure of a girl but the face of an old woman, and her long gray hair fell loose over her shoulders. The woman was moving toward him, but her feet hovered a few inches above the floor. The carpenter plastered himself against the wall in fright, but the ghost kept coming toward him. The ghost was directly between the carpenter and the open trapdoor, and the carpenter knew he'd have to run right through her to get out. Then he noticed that her body was starting to fade. Summoning all his courage, the carpenter flung himself right through the ghost and leapt down through the trapdoor to the second-floor hallway. He gave a loud shout for his workers, and they all roared off in the truck, leaving their work undone.

The carpenter explained what had happened to the caretaker when he reluctantly came back to finish the job. This time, he decided to work on the exterior of the house until he was sure it was safe to go back inside. There was scraping and painting to be done, and one of the attic windows had broken when a ladder fell against it. He could do that repair from the scaffolding outside, though he dreaded the thought of going into that haunted attic to clean up the shattered glass.

The carpenter was almost finished with the window repair when he glanced inside the attic and saw the ghost hovering on the other side of the glass, peering out at him. He sucked in a breath and stared intently at the figure to make sure he wasn't imagining it. Yes, a woman wearing a flowing floor-length dress was hovering a few inches above the floorboards. He could see shattered glass below her feet. The carpenter made good time exiting the scaffolding and even better time departing the premises, never to return.

"It was a good thing the repairs were pretty much done by that point," said the wife. "But here's the real kicker! The carpenter never told us about the broken glass in the attic. We woke up that night hearing sweeping sounds in the attic, but we had no idea the ghost was tidying up until we went upstairs the next day and found the broken glass shards swept into a pile, ready for disposal."

My daddy was impressed. "I wonder if the ghost would hire herself out for some light housekeeping duties. My apartment is a mess!"

All three chuckled at the joke. It helped to dispel the supernatural chill the caretaker's story had evoked in all of them. At that moment, a family entered the dining room, so my daddy excused himself and went to take their orders.

Caretakers have come and gone since my daddy's college days, and still the ghost of Rue wanders the house and grounds of Heceta Head, floating up the steps, tidying the house, peering sadly out to sea and once even putting out a kitchen fire that threatened to burn down the home she guards.

I've never met her myself, but on days like today when I stand up by the lighthouse looking out over the sea, sometimes the wind in my ears sounds like the sigh of a sad mother mourning the loss of her child. And when I look up toward the attic window in the keeper's house, I often wonder if the glint of light on the glass is just the sparkle of sunshine — or could it be Rue?

15

The Empty Chair

ASHLAND

My wife and I are theater buffs, and Shakespeare is a particular passion for us. We read the plays aloud to each other while we were courting, and after our wedding, we honeymooned in Great Britain so we could attend several plays at the Globe Theatre and a few more at the Royal Shakespeare Theatre in Stratford-upon-Avon. When I am in a teasing mood, I often call my wife "Beatrice" after a character in *Much Ado About Nothing*.

In fact, Shakespeare is the reason we chose to live in Ashland instead of buying a house in Medford, where my wife's family had settled. A young chap from Southern Oregon Normal School started the Oregon Shakespeare Festival back in 1935. By the time my wife and I bought our house in Ashland, it was a well-established tradition. We particularly loved the Elizabethan Theater, an open-air theater with 1,200 seats. Attending plays there always reminded us of our honeymoon.

Pretty early on, my wife and I started mixing it up a bit, going to live theater productions whenever we could and to the movies when we couldn't. My wife became a big fan of British actor Charles Laughton after he came to America to make films.

We saw them all: *Mutiny on the Bounty*, *The Hunchback of Notre Dame*, *Hobson's Choice*, *Witness for the Prosecution*. I could go on and on.

In the early 1960s, we started hearing rumors that Angus L. Bowmer, the producing director of the Shakespeare Festival, was hoping to persuade Charles Laughton to act in one of the plays. My wife was so excited she could barely sit still when she conveyed the rumor to me over dinner.

"Can you imagine?" she repeated over and over. "Charles Laughton. Here in Ashland!"

I was skeptical at first. It seemed a bit farfetched. But then— holy cow—we spotted the actor himself attending one of the performances. I thought my wife would faint! We heard from friends closely connected to the theater that the actor attended four Shakespeare productions in a row and actually delayed one of his films so he could take in the performances. Apparently, he told Angus Bowmer, "I have just seen the four best productions of Shakespeare that I have ever seen in my life."

My wife started her litany all over again when she heard this news. "Can you imagine? Charles Laughton said that. About *our festival*. Charles Laughton!"

Our inside source also claimed that Laughton begged Bowmer for a chance to play the lead role in *King Lear* after he finished filming his next movie. And Bowmer agreed. I figured we'd be seeing that particular play more than once, so I started a *King Lear* budget to make sure my obsessed wife could see the play as often as she liked. Maybe we'd bring the grandkids to a performance or two while we were at it.

What we didn't know was that Laughton was battling kidney cancer. He died on December 15, 1962, before he could return to Ashland to act in *King Lear.* My wife cried when she heard the news. Our insider friend told me privately that Laughton had also been considering the role of Falstaff in *The Merry Wives of Windsor.* I decided not to mention this to my wife. She was already disconsolate over *King Lear.*

The Merry Wives of Windsor was staged the season following Laughton's death, and I made sure we got tickets to the performance. I'd been hearing some strange rumors about the rehearsals. Some of the actors and actresses claimed they felt a presence backstage. This impression grew more pronounced as the show got underway. A great bellow of laughter would ring out occasionally from an empty part of the stage, and the cast claimed it sounded just like Charles Laughton when he laughed aloud in *The Private Life of Henry VIII.* I even heard rumors that the ghost of the British actor had appeared backstage wearing the costume of Falstaff. My wife and I sat right up front during *The Merry Wives of Windsor,* the better to watch for a ghostly presence, but we didn't hear Charles Laughton laughing or see an extra Falstaff striding around in the wings.

King Lear was staged the next year. As a tribute to our favorite British actor, I hauled out the money I'd stashed away for the occasion and purchased tickets for the whole family— kids, grandkids, and a cousin who was visiting from out-of-town.

When the big night arrived, we dressed to the nines and splurged on dinner at a fancy restaurant before driving to the theater. Our cousin was called away to an emergency during dinner, so there was an empty chair beside my wife when we took our place among the crowd.

The stage was set and the audience excited. As the first scene opened, my wife jumped and turned to stare at the empty chair

THE EMPTY CHAIR

beside her, her eyes wide with surprise. I nudged her gently, and she whispered, "Someone is sitting there. I heard a sigh."

I stared at the empty chair and felt chills crawl up my arms. Could it be possible? Could the spirit of Charles Laughton be sitting beside us? According to the cast, he'd appeared during *The Merry Wives of Windsor*, and that role was an afterthought. The role he really wanted to play was *King Lear*—and King Lear had just made his first appearance on stage.

As the play progressed, I became more and more convinced that we were sharing our row with a ghost. The air above the empty chair seemed to shimmer whenever I glanced at it. And a slight buzzing noise—almost a low hum—could be heard.

The action on stage grew more fevered. The plot thickened and thickened again. The buzzing sound intensified with each twist of the plot. People in front of us kept turning around, and several shushed us, even though we weren't speaking. Eventually, the buzzing grew so loud that everyone in the section was straining their necks, trying to locate the source of the sound. Suddenly, the shimmering air and the loud buzzing sound coalesced into a translucent ball that rose above our heads and made its way toward the stage. At that moment, I wished I was psychic so I could see the ghost that was creating all the buzz.

The wide-eyed cast valiantly kept speaking their lines as the buzzing presence joined them on the boards. Professionals all, they finished the scene before fleeing backstage to compose themselves. The buzzing sound abated with the scene.

The audience was flabbergasted. What had just happened? Had the spirit of Charles Loughton just commandeered the stage for one last performance?

The play swept along to its dramatic conclusion. When King Lear appeared onstage, bearing the body of his beloved daughter Cordelia, a soft sigh sounded from the empty chair beside my wife. Unbeknownst to us, our unseen companion had returned to our row.

And then the play was over. As the crowd applauded, the shimmer over the empty chair dissipated. The ghost was gone. On the way home, the grandkids couldn't stop talking about the buzzing sound that had disrupted the performance. Everyone believed it was the ghost of Charles Laughton who had taken the stage for one final bow. It would be a story to tell over and over again for the rest of our lives.

"Well, my dear," I said to my wife as we readied ourselves for bed that night. "I believe you just got your wish. You got to see Charles Laughton on stage at our Shakespeare festival."

My wife laughed a bit shakily. "I think you are right. But I hope that next time around he finds another place to sit!"

PART TWO
Powers of Darkness and Light

16

Devil's Lake

In my father's father's day, our people lived beside a beautiful lake near the sea. We hunted and fished, laughed, loved, and died upon its shores. The land was good to us, and we to it. We never took more than we gave, and we were thankful for what the spirits provided us. My grandfather never understood why such a trial was sent to us, and I confess that I feel the same. We were a good people. We did not deserve what happened.

In that time, we were led by a mighty warrior with one son—Great Bear. Great Bear was the handsomest, strongest, and most agile of all the young men in the village, and all the maidens vied for his attention. All but one. She was called Small Faun, the daughter of the medicine man, and she was beautiful, with flowing dark hair, limpid black eyes with golden sparkles, and a rosebud mouth made for kisses and smiles. Small Faun had a head full of knowledge, and she was considered a wise woman—something unheard of for one so young. But she seemed to naturally know the secrets of the world around her, to understand the voices of the birds and the words of the sea lapping at the shore, and to speak the language of the seals and sea lions that swam in its waters.

Great Bear was fascinated by the young girl. When he was fishing, he watched her as she strolled the banks of the lake. When hunting, he deliberately carried his prized elk or bear or deer past her house. Here was one, he silently told her, who will provide for your every need. But still she did not smile on him as did the other maidens, and Great Bear began to fear that she hated him for killing her beloved creatures. But he misjudged Small Faun, for she understood that life is a circle, that death and life are intertwined.

One day, Great Bear decided to fish in the sea, and he carried his nets down to the ocean a few miles from the village. There, he found Small Faun seated beside a large sea lion, listening as it grunted at her. He stood a few yards away, watching in fascination. "What does he say to you?" he murmured under his breath, knowing she would not hear. But Small Faun answered him at once. "He tells me of swimming in the sea, and the big fish he caught this morning. He is proud of that fish. It tasted very good to him."

Fascinated, Great Bear sat down where he was and watched as Small Faun spoke to the sea lion and it spoke back. Then the great creature waddled back into the foaming sea. Small Faun sighed and stood up. And for the first time, she smiled at Great Bear. Hands trembling and heart pounding fiercely, he smiled back.

From that day on, Great Bear often found himself walking with Small Faun beside the seashore or the lake, listening as she taught him the ways of the small creatures that abounded in their woodland home. And Small Faun started watching for Great Bear when he was out hunting or fishing or making canoes. And her heart beat faster and her hands trembled whenever he looked up from his work and smiled at her.

They were married at midsummer, and the whole tribe rejoiced in the match. About a month after the marriage took place, Great Bear entered his new lodge after a fruitless day of hunting to find his bride pale and shaking with fear.

"What is it?" he asked, catching her in his arms. "What's wrong?"

"I do not know," Small Faun cried, burying her dark head against his shoulder. "The animals all tell me that something terrible comes, but they do not know what it is. They all run and hide now when I approach, and many are leaving this place."

"Perhaps that is why all the hunters returned empty-handed today," Great Bear mused. "Do you think it is another Long Storm approaching our shore?" A few years previously, a storm from the sea had raged for four days. The lake waters rose, flooding their village, and the winds had torn apart many homes and thrown down mighty trees. Many villagers had died.

"I do not sense a storm coming, and the sea lions do not report any of the usual signs they see when bad weather washes ashore," she replied. "All I know is that something comes that strikes terror into my heart and makes all the creatures of nature afraid."

"What can we do?" asked Great Bear.

"I think we should speak to my father and yours, and see if they can divine what is frightening the animals," Small Faun said. "In the meantime, I will go ask the owl when dusk falls. Of all the creatures, he is the wisest in the ways of our land, and he has lived a long time."

Great Bear agreed to this plan and went at once to speak to the chief and medicine man about what Small Faun had learned. The medicine man at once retreated to his lodge—so recently vacated by his lovely daughter—and began the rituals of divination. Great Bear's father, the chief, had more practical matters in mind.

"If the animals are fleeing from this land, we may shortly be wanting for food, my son," he said. "Take a few of the best fishers in the village and go out on the lake to see what may be caught there. I do not want anyone to go hungry."

Great Bear did as his father bid, gathering together several men and setting out on the lake with nets and spears. Dusk was settling over the gleaming lake as they set forth. The lake was uncannily still. Great Bear noticed the stillness with a shudder. Surely something was wrong in this place. But what?

They were aiming for the opposite shore, which had many shallows and was a favorite fishing place. Great Bear's canoe neared the center of the lake, which was churning slightly, as if under the force of a breeze, though no wind was blowing. Great Bear stared at the bubbles and waves, puzzled, when he heard a voice calling faintly on the wind. He glanced behind him and saw Small Faun running frantically down toward the shore from the woods, waving her arms to call him back. And that was when the bow of Great Bear's canoe was smashed open by a huge tentacle that shot up from the depths of the lake. More tentacles appeared, ripping the wooden boat to pieces. Great Bear was pitched out of the canoe into the water with a shout of astonished fear. Faintly, before the water closed over his head, he heard Small Faun scream.

When Great Bear's head broke the surface of the lake, everything around him was in chaos. Mighty tentacles were splashing the water into waves and foam. Splinters of canoe floated everywhere, and several of his warriors were caught in the limbs of the monster and being thrashed against the water. One man at least was already dead—his neck snapped by a waving tentacle. Great Bear swam toward a long sliver of wood, hoping to use it as a spear, and came face-to-eye with the creature as its large head and beaked mouth emerged from the water. For a moment they stared at one another, mesmerized. Then Great Bear felt a tentacle wrap around his body, and he was lifted high into the air.

On shore, Small Faun's screams brought the whole village running. They watched in horror as one by one the warriors were snatched from the remains of the canoes by the monster's tentacles and thrust into its beak. Finally, sated, the monster disappeared beneath the surface of the lake. A few floating bits of wood were all that remained of the fishing party.

Small Faun could not stop screaming. The terrible cries tore from her throat, one after another, in a steady stream. It was only after her father gave her a hard shake by the shoulders that she collapsed against him and fainted. Her father carried her to his lodge, followed by weeping, exclaiming villagers. Around them, night fell. A dark night in which no bird sang, no creature rustled, no owl hooted. Everyone and everything was still, hiding from the monster in the lake.

The next morning, the chief packed up his people and moved the whole village inland, away from the deadly waters. But Small Faun slipped away as the people were loading up their belongings and took one of the canoes out to the center of the lake. Her father missed her almost at once, and—guessing her intent—ran to the shore of the lake. He was just in time to see a tentacle shoot out of the water and wrap itself around canoe and girl. Then both vanished silently under the bubbling waters.

DEVIL'S LAKE

As soon as the villagers were safely inland, a great funeral was held for the dead warriors and for Small Faun, who could not bear to be parted from her husband, even in death. And the lake was avoided by that generation and the next. It is only now that we go back, sometimes, to fish on its waters. But still, we call it "Devil's Lake," and all who fish there drop an offering into its depths to appease the creature who lies below in wait.

17

The Lights

HELLS CANYON

I've lived my whole life in the Canyon, just about. I raised Cain when I was a young boy, played sports in high school, wooed my pretty girl and married her, and finally settled down in a house overlooking the reservoir and got a job at a local business. The canyon walls were my home. Sometimes visitors asked me if I didn't want to get out into the wide world and travel. Maybe move to the East Coast. But I tried life outside the canyon once, and it wasn't for me. I like living in a place where you know most everyone in town and they know you. Where the wild things roam at will, and nature is just one more force you live with. My family is here, and so is my heart. That's why I stay.

Being a lifetime resident, I know all the stories about this place. All the high jinks and pranks pulled by the local kids. The crazy, funny, scary stories about elk and cougar and bighorn sheep. I even heard the ghost of a baby crying once when I was visiting a local cemetery to look for historic gravestones—scared me pretty bad, standing among the tombstones in broad daylight while the voice of a baby fretted and wailed mournfully over my left shoulder. I asked folks about the ghost, but no one

THE LIGHTS

knew who the baby was or why it cried. There were a couple of small tombstones in that vicinity belonging to little ones, but no indication of which child was weeping.

Anyhow, I know most things about Hells Canyon, and I even live in a place of secrets: a house built on an old mining claim that was considered a sacred place by the Nez Perce tribe. It was one of the very first frame houses in this area, and folks like to call it the "mansion," though by today's standards it's just an ordinary house. But the grounds were far from ordinary. Above the house was a spring and a cave full of petroglyphs, and one of the women from the local tribe told me her people used to mine the cave for sacred crystals. The crystals were said to glow with a purplish light after being charged in the sun, and the light was held to last well into the nighttime. There were also turquoise stones in the cave that the tribe would grind to make green and blue paint. And when I was digging a garden in the yard, I uncovered a large rock the size of a table. It was flat on one side and had a tracing of a human figure. But never once did I find an arrowhead or an object of war in that place, though arrowheads were abundant on either side of the property.

The only thing I hadn't seen in the canyon was the phenomenon we locals call "the lights." My friends had seen them more than once over the reservoir at night and had described them in detail. There were three amber lights forming a triangle—one on each point—and two more on either side of the triangle, as if they were escorting it. People traveling on the road beside the Oxbow Reservoir would see the lights appear just below the mountaintops and travel along at the same speed of the car—thirty or forty miles per hour. Sometimes the lights would follow the car, starting and stopping when it started and stopped, although after awhile they would turn and disappear over the mountain. The lights never made a sound.

There were many theories about the lights, of course. UFOs, or spirit lights, some folks thought. A secret scientific experiment by the government, said others. I sometimes wondered if it might not be the spirits or guardians of the canyon that were once honored by the Nez Perce at the sacred place behind my house. No one knew the answer, just like no one knew about the ghost-baby who cried in the cemetery. We just accepted the lights as another fact of life in Hells Canyon and kept on living our lives.

I was a bit frustrated at being the only one who hadn't seen the lights. I started watching for them every night after I closed up the restaurant and drove home. Was that a glimmer at the top of the canyon? No, just an early star. Night after night I sighed, parked the car, and went inside.

The week it happened, I was all alone. My wife and baby were off visiting her folks. One night, I sat on the porch by myself, looking out over the reservoir in search of the amber lights. But before long, I got to feeling lonesome and took myself inside to bed.

Sometime later I woke up with a start, heart beating fast, not sure what had awakened me. My room was bathed with an eerie amber light that cast strange shadows all over the walls. The light blazed in from the window beside the bed, and I knew at once that there must be a wildfire somewhere on the hills. I ran from the room and out onto the porch, wanting to get an accurate location to phone in to the fire department. But there was no smell of burning, no crackle of flames, and no massive firelight on the horizon. From the porch, I couldn't even see the amber blaze that had lit the back bedroom. That gave me goose bumps. If the light wasn't caused by a wildfire, than what was it? My legs were shaking as I returned to my room and saw the light still glowing through the window. The amber light blinked off and on several times, as if something were moving around high in the air. My heart leapt in my chest and started to pound. This was it: my chance to see the lights up close and personal. If I could force my shaking legs to walk! I hadn't reckoned on feeling so completely overwhelmed.

Slowly, I went out the back door, looked up, and saw it. A triangle of amber lights hovering just under the mountaintop with two escort lights, one on either side of the object. I stood motionless, filled in equal parts with fear and wonder. What was it? Straining my ears, I was sure I heard a faint hum, almost like the sound of a Geiger counter. Then the lights turned suddenly and disappeared over the mountaintop, gone in the blink of an eye.

I slowly went back inside and slipped into bed, but I was too excited to sleep. I'd seen them! I'd seen the lights.

I was dozing when they returned, filling the room again with amber brilliance. I went out to see them, but as soon as I set foot outside they zipped across the reservoir and disappeared above the mountains. After that, I remained in my bed and just watched as the amber lights came and went, flickering across the sheetrock walls, growing bright, dimming, flickering, and finally disappearing. The lights hovered nearby for about forty-five minutes before the solid darkness of night finally settled over my house.

I've seen the lights a couple more times since then. Once in a while the amber glow brightens the walls of my bedroom as the lights pass overhead. And one time I saw them keeping pace with a passing car driving alongside the Oxbow Reservoir at night. I always get goose bumps when they appear and am filled again with fear and wonder.

Of course, at local gatherings, all the residents like to speculate endlessly about the source of the lights. I rarely participate. I just listen. I don't claim to understand what the lights are. I just feel privileged to have seen them.

18

Trespassing

CASCADE MOUNTAINS

They'll tell you all hunters have stories about strange encounters in the wild. And they'd be right. But I'd bet my last dollar that you haven't heard a story quite like mine. I'm an old man now, and I was just a young chap newly married when it happened. But I remember the whole incident, clear as day, and it still makes my knees shake and my belly turn over with fear, fifty-odd years later.

A pal of mine and I were avid hunters and trappers back in those days. Every three or four months we'd head up into the mountains together to lay traps, hoping to bring home a good-sized elk or bear for our families to eat. Albert and I were in high spirits that early autumn day as we gathered up our guns and replacement traps and the other gear we needed. We packed everything onto Molly, my pack mule, and headed into the Cascades, talking cheerfully and singing old songs, guns held in a cocksure manner over our shoulders. We'd placed our traps in a new stream during our last trip, and we were going to search out a new campsite nearby. Daring explorers, we called ourselves, and Albert started calling me "Lewis" after the famed Lewis and Clark, the real daring explorers who'd first come to Oregon so long ago and built a fort up in Astoria near the mouth of the Columbia.

We marched eastward and southward for three days, approaching our destination from the north. Then we walked right past our usual campsite and made our way along the new stream we'd located on our last trip, setting traps as we passed. We made our way eastward, seeking a nice place to erect the tent-camp that would be our home away from home for a couple of weeks. We found a place we liked eventually—a sort of round clearing among a huge stand of Douglas fir. These were just about the largest trees I'd ever seen, though Albert— who'd been to California—claimed to have seen even bigger sequoia down there. Green moss dripped from their limbs, and a small cascade to the west of us kept the air moist. Vines and a few smaller trees circled the edges of the clearing where sunlight had managed to break through the massive firs just long enough to give them light to grow. It was a peaceful spot, and strangely quiet. I couldn't hear any birds chirping or see any scurrying, though chipmunks and other little creatures had been very evident just a few miles back.

"We'd better put up the tents right away," Albert said briskly, starting to untie the packs on Molly's sturdy back. "The temperature's dropping, and there's going to be an early snow, or my name ain't Albert!"

I shrugged and helped with the packs. Albert had a genius for predicting the weather, and when he said it would snow, I believed him. We'd come ready, knowing how unpredictable the weather could be when you were five-thousand-plus feet above sea level and still climbing. I started assembling the tents and shivered a bit as the sharp metallic sound of hammer hitting tent spike broke the uncanny stillness. I wasn't sure I liked this clearing, now that I'd spent some time here. How had such a space come about among all the tall trees? Usually we camped out in the openings between the Douglas fir and Sitka spruce that lined the slopes. This clearing was unusual, in my experience, and I wondered uneasily if it was a sacred place to the native tribes that once populated this region. Some of the boulders at the far edge of the clearing were made of glassy black obsidian. They were piled atop one another in such an organized manner that they seemed to make a monument of some sort. *Or a tomb*, my subconscious added. My hands started to shake and—sure enough—the hammer missed its spike and hit my thumb instead. I gave a shout of pain, dropped the hammer, and started jumping up and down, shaking my hand as if I could wave the pain away. I wanted to curse but didn't dare disturb the sacred hush around me.

Albert laughed, not seeming to feel the sacredness of this spot at all. He cussed and fumed as he always did while tethering Molly out to eat her fill of the tallish grass in the clearing. Then he put up his tent and assembled the ropes we would need to hang our trapped game—when we got some—from the tall firs, so as to discourage bears. His matter-of-fact attitude should have calmed my feeling of uneasiness, but in truth, it helped not a whit. For the first time ever, I felt a stranger in these tall, wild mountains, and I was very much aware of our isolation. Not another soul lived in this desolate spot, and none could be reached within fifty miles of here, should we need help. I shuddered again at the thought, astonished at how upset I felt the longer I stayed here. Thrusting aside my morbid musings, I finished putting up my own small sleeping tent, constructed a small lean-to to store our hunting, trapping, and fishing gear, and then skinned a rabbit that Albert had shot earlier that day and set it cooking over a campfire. I found the sizzling smell of the meat cheering and thrust a can of beans to cook in the coals beside it.

Dusk had already fallen around us, coming earlier now that it was autumn. It was helped along by the shadows of the massive trees. Albert settled next to the fire with a happy sigh and then cussed when he sat on a prickly pinecone. To our right, Molly made little sound as she cropped the grass. She was sticking to the edge of the clearing close to our tents, I noticed, rather than eating the thicker grass in the center. It seemed as if she too were nervous, though I had more than once labeled Molly as the most placid beast that ever lived.

"Don't cuss so much," I said sharply, even though I wasn't guilt-free in this department myself—at least on a normal trip.

"Why not?" Albert demanded, pulling out his pipe and starting to fill it with tobacco.

"'Cause this is a sacred place," I snapped. "Can't you sense it? There's a hush over this clearing, and I think that's a monument of some sort." I gestured to the boulders on the far side, barely visible now in the growing darkness. They loomed menacingly against the lighter gray of the sky, and from this angle they resembled the twisted figure of a man, poised to strike at anyone trespassing on his domain. I said as much to Albert, and he laughed heartily. "Just your imagination, Ben," he said.

"I'd still be happier if we found someplace else to camp," I said stubbornly, flipping the meat over in the pan. "I don't like this place."

"This is the perfect place," Albert retorted, lighting his pipe and settling down to smoke. "Don't be a ninny."

I frowned and then yelped as I burnt myself trying to adjust the bean-can deeper among the coals. Above us, the wind hissed softly through the firs like a chorus of rattlers shaking a warning. Storm clouds roiled overhead, blotting out the last of the stars, and snowflakes started falling softly around us as I piled meat onto two plates, filling the empty spots with baked beans. The food was hot and tasted good. It did much to raise my spirits. For a few moments, the shadows flickering outside the small campfire seemed a little less dark, a little less hostile. Full night had come and blotted away everything except the falling snow, the firs behind our tents, and the cheerful crackle of the fire. I wished that the firelight would penetrate more of the darkness surrounding us. I was very aware of the dark boulders on the far side of the clearing, though they were invisible now. *Trespassers*, they seemed to say accusingly. Above my head, the wind tossed the fir trees violently, making them creak and shake like hands writhing in pain.

"Time for bed," Albert said at last, laying aside his plate, knife, and fork. He banked down the fire while I washed up our few dishes in the bucket of water I'd brought from the stream. I'd made the short journey to water's edge with many a hesitating look around me at the looming trees and gently falling snow, cursing myself silently for a fool. The forest had never frightened me before. I checked on Molly when I finished washing up. For some reason, she had chosen to sleep huddled behind the tents rather than under the massive Douglas firs of the forest. Glancing into the too-silent clearing, I didn't blame her a bit.

Albert had already gone into his tent, and I could hear him shuffling around inside, making himself comfortable. I crawled into my own tent and huddled down to sleep on some softish fir branches I'd gathered and covered with blankets. I tossed and turned for a long time, remembering the boulder monument that looked like a twisted man on the other side of the clearing. What I hadn't said to Albert—and wished fervently I hadn't seen—was the sudden addition of a second head to the monument, there one minute and gone the next. A head with yellow eyes that gleamed red in the firelight. Finally, I got a grip on my lacerated nerves, told myself firmly that I'd seen a coyote or a wildcat of some sort, and forced myself to lie still. On the edge of sleep, I realized vaguely that the second figure I'd seen would have had to have been more than seven feet tall to peer over the stones. Then darkness descended and I slept.

I awoke once in the night, pulse hammering in my neck and wrists, sure I'd heard something. A frightened bray? The whistle of the wind in the trees? A heavy footfall? As my eyes adjusted to the darkness inside my small tent, I thought I saw a darker shape looming above the gray dimness that was the roof of the shelter. It had the twisted shape of a large man. For a moment, I smelled a dusky, ancient smell like dead leaves and sweat and moldy bread and dust. Then smell and shadow were gone so quickly I might have imagined them. But the painful slam of my heart against my ribs and the gasping breaths I took to calm myself told a different story. I'd definitely seen something— and it wasn't human. I reached for my gun, glad I'd chosen to sleep with it beside me. The feel of the barrel against my hand brought some relief from my fear and from my terrible sense of isolation. Three days' walk back to civilization. For a moment I thought of Molly, tethered outside behind the tents—trapped between us and the trees. But I heard no frightened braying and decided that the danger had passed.

I woke early the next morning to a world already warming. The light snow was melting rapidly, and the clearing, though still silent, was sunny and almost inviting. I gave a cheerful yell to wake up Albert and glanced around for Molly. And realized then why I hadn't heard her in the night. The tether had broken and Molly was gone; had fled from the too-silent clearing with its menacing monument of black obsidian. I yelled for Albert again, a note of panic in my voice, and stared into the rapidly melting snow around the edges of our camp, which was trampled down as if a large beast had been pacing back and forth for much of the night. Albert crashed out of the entrance to his tent, dark hair wild and eyes still sleepy. But they sharpened at once when he saw the remains of the animal tracks in the snow and whistled through his teeth.

"Woo-eee," he said. "That looks like a mighty big bear! We've got some good hunting to do today, Benny-boy! This one's a prize-winner, or my name ain't Albert McGee!"

I nodded mutely, clutching my rifle in shaking hands. The melting tracks didn't look like bear to me. One of them looked like the footprint of a giant man. I'd heard stories about a wild creature, a half-man, half-beast called a *Sasquatch* that was rumored to roam the Cascades, but I'd put it down to myth. Until I saw that footprint. As I stared at it, a glob of melting snow caved in, ruining the shape. Too late to show it to Albert.

"We should go after Molly," I said instead. "I don't hanker to carry all that gear out on my back."

"She'll be back soon enough," Albert said. "She won't have run far from camp. We'd best go after the bear that frightened her."

We compromised, making a wide swing around camp calling for Molly, who was nowhere to be seen. One or two hoof prints in the snowy mud showed us she'd headed in the direction of our old campsite. Albert clapped me on the back and said: "See, Ben? Told you there was nothing to worry about. We can pick Molly up at our old site on our way home. But first, let's get that bear! Hunting's what we came to do, so let's do it!"

Grabbing some cold meat and bread to chew as we walked, we headed downstream in the direction Albert reckoned the "bear" had taken. I was glad to stick to the woods, far away from that eerie clearing with its looming tomb-like monolith of shiny black stone. Albert had brought the last two traps with him, and we set them at likely spots further downstream, keeping a sharp lookout for the giant bear that had frightened Molly and paced around our camp. We saw nothing, not even a squirrel or a chipmunk. Sometimes the rustle of wings could be heard far up in the branches of the huge trees around us, but nothing else. The sun occasionally ventured a dappled ray or two through the thick, moss-covered branches and made pretty leaf-patterns on massive trunks or on the needle-strewn earth. I would have enjoyed the sight if it weren't for the uncanny silence and the feeling I sometimes had of being watched.

Thankfully, this feeling faded away as we got further from our camp in the sacred clearing. But it returned when we finally called it quits and headed back, hurrying because dusk came early in the thick mountain forest. We hadn't shot a single thing, and both traps were empty as we passed them on our way upstream. The feeling of being followed grew, making my skin prick and my body shake. I grew so jumpy that Albert caught my anxiety and grumbled at me for making him act like an idiot.

As we neared the clearing, I caught a familiar metallic smell. Pungent and gut-wrenching, it was, and it took me a moment to recognize it. Blood. I gasped and ran forward, then, Albert on my heels, clutching my rifle fiercely, the safety off. I skidded to a halt beneath a massive Douglas fir on the edge of the clearing. In the dimness of twilight, I looked on a scene of terrible destruction. The tents had been ripped from their anchors, pots and pans were strewn everywhere, fishing gear was tangled about, and Molly's dead body lay atop her saddlebags, her head almost twisted off and her still-steaming blood spattered over everything. It was obvious that she was newly killed and that the creature who had destroyed the camp only recently departed.

"A bear never did this," Albert said in a high-pitched voice quite unlike his own. His blue eyes bulged with horror as he stared at poor Molly.

"No," I agreed, equally shaken.

I felt invisible eyes glaring at me from the direction of the black monument on the far side of the clearing, and I wanted to flee as fast as my wobbly legs could go. But the woods were already dark, and the dangers that lay in scrambling through the mountains at night were worse than those that faced us in this clearing. We had our guns, and we could build a fire big enough to keep whatever creature had done this at bay until the sun rose and we could safely make our escape. I said as much to Albert, confirming what he had been thinking himself. We skirted the body of the mule and grabbed blankets from the ruined tents. Then we built a huge bonfire in front of the lean-to, miraculously still intact, and settled down for the night wrapped in blankets with our backs to the tree. Above us, the roof of the lean-to blotted out the stars, which seemed remote and peaceful in this horrible clearing. I expected the smell of blood to bring a bear or a cougar during the night, but no creature, large or small, ventured into the clearing. I lay awake, too tense to sleep, my hands always on my gun, and from the occasional gleam I saw from his open eyes, I knew Albert too was awake. Once, I thought I saw a movement out beyond the lean-to and the bonfire. It was a tall shape almost like that of a man, though the shoulders were too broad, the arms too long. It appeared and disappeared so swiftly I wasn't sure if I'd really seen it. I shuddered and said nothing to Albert.

As soon as daylight came, Albert and I were up and cleaning our gear. Suddenly, Albert reared back on his heels and stared at me. "The traps! We left two traps downstream," he said urgently. "I don't aim to come here ever again, and I ain't leaving without my traps. You run down and grab them while I finish up here, Benny-boy!"

"They're your traps," I protested. "You go get them if you want them. I just want to pack up our things and get out of here. I'll buy you two new traps when we get home."

"I pack faster than you," Albert said. "By the time you get back with the traps, I'll be done here and we can leave."

"It's safer if we stay together," I protested.

"That critter's long gone by now," Albert said. "And we've both got our guns. Why buy new traps when we don't have to? Come on! Get a move on and get them traps. That way we don't have to backtrack before getting out of here."

Reluctantly, I agreed. Holding tight to my gun, I hurried away from the sacred clearing with its grisly mess and ominous black monument and headed into the woods. The stream was burbling gently, and as I moved downstream, I heard a few tentative calls from birds overhead. The feeling of fear and menace faded a bit, and I stopped shaking. I quickly became absorbed in my task. We'd gotten a beaver in the second trap, and I felt almost elated at the sight. Albert would be pleased. And, even better than the beaver, we were getting out of this terrible place and heading back to our base camp.

So eager was I to leave that I almost ran back to camp. I skirted a massive Douglas fir and stepped into the sunlit clearing, expecting to see Albert standing there with two packed bags, ready to go. I saw the packs at once, only a few feet away. And nearby, Molly's body was now decently covered with the fir branches we'd used as bedding the first night. But where was Albert? My skin went clammy, and I was again aware of the silence, the menacing black rocks, and invisible eyes staring at me, willing me to go.

"Not without Albert," I said aloud to the invisible eyes that were watching me, my whole body trembling with fear. "I know this is a sacred place, and I promise to leave it alone forever after this. But I won't leave without my friend."

Then I saw the butt of a rifle sticking out from behind one of the branches covering Molly. I dropped the traps, but not my gun, and willed myself forward one step at a time, until I saw Albert lying on the far side of the dead mule. His face was white as a sheet, his eyes staring sightlessly upward, and his head was at an awkward angle, as if his neck had been snapped. He hadn't even had time to fire a shot. The creature must have come up from behind him while he was working over Molly.

TRESPASSING

I drew in several ragged breaths then knelt beside the body and lifted Albert onto my shoulder while still holding my rifle ready—not an easy task. Then I took up the other rifle and stumbled out of the clearing, feeling the beast watching me. As I departed, I glanced once toward the black-glassy monument and saw a tall figure, almost eight feet high, with a twisted, ape-like countenance. It had a massive torso and long arms and was covered with brown hair. I was vulnerable in that moment. It could have killed me in one murderous rush. But it didn't. It let me go, carrying my dead friend.

It took me nearly a week to walk out of the mountains with Albert. I had left everything behind but the rifles, and I paused only once each day to shoot something to eat, though I had to stop at night or risk pitching over a cliff in the darkness. But I made it at last, delivering Albert's body to his family before going home to my wife. The doctor called in to examine Albert's body estimated that the creature who killed him must have had enormous strength and been at least seven feet tall. Which matched the description of the Sasquatch I'd seen in the clearing. He said I'd had a lucky escape, which was true. But I sometimes wondered if I'd been spared because I'd treated the clearing with fear and respect, calling it a sacred place and refusing to curse even when provoked. I'll never know for sure why my life was spared, but one thing at least was certain: I never went hunting in the Cascades again.

19

Tommy Knockin'

JOHN DAY

When they discovered gold along the Rogue and Umpqua Rivers, it brought gold fever to Oregon in a big way. Up until then, Oregonians had been abandoning their jobs to rush down to California and dig for gold. Now Californians and other folks were coming here. Miners, merchants, and scoundrels of all sorts flooded into southern Oregon. The native tribes fought with the miners over their land but were eventually forced out as new roads were graded and boomtowns sprung up hither and yon. But the mines played out after a few years, and we figured that was that. Settlers, farmers, and loggers moved into the Rogue and Umpqua River Valleys, and folks were sure that Oregon had yielded up all her gold.

Then news came from the East. Gold had been discovered in the Blue Mountains near the John Day River and Union Flat. Miners and gold seekers poured into the area, and hard-rock mines and prospect shafts were sunk throughout the region. In the vicinity of Sumpter, an entire valley was dredged and sluiced in search of gold.

Now I'll admit that I had gold fever as much as the next man. I was one of the first to set foot in the boomtown that

TOMMY KNOCKIN'

became known as John Day—I and my mule Bessy, that is, who went everywhere with me. I was hoping to make my fortune in the gold fields, and it looked as if that hope would be fulfilled. It was hard work—Jehoshaphat, but it was! Digging down into darkness, searching with smoky candles and lanterns for the elusive mother lode of gold, training mules to walk into dark holes and haul out wagonloads of gold-laced quartz. It was a relief to get home at night and spend time drinking in the tavern or doing a little gambling with a poke of gold dust.

I soon made friends with a couple of Chinese fellows who set up shop in the area. My grandma had been to the Far East with her sea-captain husband, and she was a firm believer in Chinese medicine. When I busted an arm in a minor cave-in, the first thing I did, after the ding-dang doctor who set the arm let me get out of bed, was to head down to the Chinese grocery and ask the fellow there for some of his medicines. It was a smallish building, smelling of opium and herbs. The Chinese medico was delighted by my request. His shop was mostly patronized by his fellow Chinese workers. Very few of the miners bought his wares, so I was a novelty.

At first, the other patrons of the store gave me strange looks, but when I started talking about my grandparent's travels to the Far East, and the places they'd visited, the atmosphere thawed out. The Chinese doc mixed up his medicines in a little room where he kept dozens of his labeled bottles full of spices and strange things like rhino horn and snake's head. He listened intently to me and asked an occasional question. I tried not to notice what foul-smelling things he was grinding up for my cure. It made me queasy to think of it. But, according to my grandma, Chinese medicine was powerful, and I was willing

131

to try anything that would get me back to mining as soon as possible.

Well, it was indeed foul-tasting stuff. But it worked. And I got more than a cure from that first visit. I also got a partner to help me in the mine. I noticed as soon as I got to the grocery that there was another white fellow in the store. He was a "Cousin Jack" from Cornwall, England, and was obviously well-known in Chinatown. He sat at a little table with a couple of other fellows, intent on mah-jongg, and didn't respond to my friendly overtures until the game was done.

I was excited to meet him. Cousin Jacks were raised as miners from the cradle up. It was a real break when you worked with one of 'em. They knew all the mining secrets, from sniffing out the wealthiest veins, to shoring up a roof so it wouldn't cave in, to the rules of behavior in a mine. To whit: no whistling, watch the rats, and honor the Tommy Knockers.

This particular Cousin Jack went by the name of Jacob Smith. He was a rugged-looking, white-haired fellow with a wiry build and wise, deep-set, dark eyes. We struck up a friendship right then and there. He'd been hurt in a California gold mine a few years back and thought he'd never work again until someone suggested Chinese medicine to him. Those miracle doctors had gotten him back on his feet lickety-split, and since then Jacob always sought out a Chinese physician wherever he settled. I couldn't blame him.

Anyhow, Jacob was new in town and looking to work in the gold fields. He was happy to sign on to my shift in the mine, and his assistance meant that I could go back to work, even with a busted arm. And it turned out that Bessy liked him, which was a plus. That ol' mule of mine was ornery as all get-out and would bite anyone she didn't like. I'd lost a couple of partners that way. They couldn't get near the wagon to load ore without Bessy taking a swipe at them, so they signed on to a different shift.

Right from the first, I was amazed at how much work Jacob got done each day. He accomplished more than twice that of the other fellows. At first, they thought he was a little odd. He always carried thick Cornish pasties in his pockets, carefully wrapped up in a handkerchief by his missus, one of the few women who came to the gold fields to keep house for her man. And he carved rough little statues of Tommy Knockers—dwarfish figures with rough leather clothes and large heads—that he propped up in crevices all along whatever shaft he was working. The Tommy Knockers were supposed to be mischievous spirits of dead miners, returned to help miners find ore and warn them of trouble, though sometimes they played tricks on folks they didn't like. Strange stuff to the practical, hard-headed Americans working this particular vein. But when the other miners saw how good he was, they forgave his quirks, and some of them begged pasties off his missus when they saw how well the food kept down in the mine.

About a month after Jacob joined us, Bessy and I drove the wagon down the shaft he was working—the task I found easiest to do with my busted arm—and chanced upon a strange scene in the flickering lamplight. Jacob was busy at one end of the shaft with timber and nails, bracing and supporting the newly blasted area so we could safely work there. At the other side of the shaft, near the little statues of the Tommy Knockers, a hammer and drill were floating in the air, working all by themselves: turn, bang, turn, bang. The drill bit deeper into the rock with each hammer stroke. And in a third part of the shaft, invisible hands were sorting through the rubble from the previous night's dynamite blast, searching for tell-tale gleams of gold. I was completely amazed, though Bessy seemed not at all disconcerted by the invisible miners.

Jacob looked up casually at me, sitting on the wagon, my mouth wide open. "That was quick," he said, giving a slight nod at the hammer and drill, which instantly stopped working and floated down to the floor.

"Wha . . . what was that?" I managed to gasp, the flesh on my arms crawling.

"Just the *Bucca*. What you Americans call Tommy Knockers," Jacob said calmly, guiding the wagon over to the rubble he wanted removed.

"They're real?" I said in astonishment. And then winced as a small rock winged out of the air and bounced off my head. "Ouch! Okay, yes I can see you are real," I called in the direction of the invisible thrower. "Sorry!"

"Better give him something to appease him, or he'll steal your tools," Jacob said as he began filling the wagon with rubble.

Another small rain of pebbles came hurling out at me as he spoke. I had often seen Jacob putting pieces of his pasty next to the small statues, and now I understood why. Hastily, I pulled a few dried apple slices from my pocket and put them by the closest statue. Immediately, the rain of pebbles ceased, and from somewhere to my left I heard a happy chuckle. Right before my eyes, the apple slices vanished.

"Don't stand there all day, lad," Jacob called. "Give me a hand here."

Still marveling at the reality of the Tommy Knockers, and a little sore about the head, I went over to help Jacob. At least, I mused, I now knew how this Cousin Jack got so much work done each day. He had assistance!

I didn't say anything to the other miners. Who would believe me? But now that I knew they existed, I saw signs of the Tommy Knockers everywhere. They took delight in stealing candles and lanterns, tossing rocks and pebbles at grumpy miners, and playing all sorts of tricks on people. They took particular delight in tapping me on the shoulder when I was busy loading up the cart, and sometimes I would hear a throaty, invisible chuckle when I jumped and whirled around. I never could get them to talk to me, although sometimes as Bessy ambled down the shaft with her load, I would hear Jacob chatting to them, and the faint sound of voices answering.

I was alone at the end of the newest shaft one morning, piling ore into Bessy's wagon, when I heard a knocking sound among the braces holding up the ceiling. This was by no means unusual. The Tommy Knockers beat upon the rafters and beams all the time to tease us. But then I heard the sound of footsteps hurrying through the cavernous rock of the mine shaft. "Ike! Ike! Get out of there!" Jacob called, his dark eyes wide with panic. I didn't ask questions. I just ran. As I did, a giant rumbling came from behind me, and the ceiling collapsed down into the tunnel, burying shaft, mule, wagon, and all. I was buried too, up to my waist, but aside from a few bruised muscles and a few cuts, I was alright, thanks to Jacob. He told me later that the Tommy Knockers had come to him with a warning, since they were not sure I would understand that—this time—their knocking was serious.

Jacob took me to the Chinese grocery, where the shopkeepers hissed in sympathy over my cuts and swollen right eye. Everyone agreed that I was lucky to be alive, and the Chinese doc got me fixed up with a couple of horrid-tasting potions that cleared the bruises and cuts up within a couple of days. That Chinese medicine was like magic! Jacob and his wife took me into their home to nurse me through my latest ailment. What with my arm still in a sling and all the battering I endured, Jacob's missus refused to let me out of bed for a week.

Guess I needed the time, too. I slept a lot, and Jacob's missus fed me up good. Still, I was in lousy spirits. I was terribly broke up about losing my mule in the cave-in. Bessy had served me well through the years, and I never knew how fond I was of the obstinate critter until she died. When I mentioned this to Jacob, he nodded in sympathy, but there was a strange look in his eyes that I couldn't interpret.

My first day back to work, I was greeted with delight by my fellow miners. I had to push the wagon along by myself that first morning. Fortunately, my arm had healed up, and I could do so without pain. Still, I knew I'd have to find a replacement for Bessy sooner or later. With a small sigh, I picked up the wagon shafts and walked into the shaft where Jacob was hard at work.

I was greeted by invisible chuckles and a small shower of pebbles. "Nice to see you too," I said politely to whatever Tommy Knockers were present. That's when I heard it. The clip-clop of hooves trotting eagerly down the shaft. Jacob looked up expectantly and grinned at me. I whirled about and saw a ghostly blue-white mule trotting toward me, over-size ears perked up and short mane bouncing jauntily in the lantern-light. Astride her back was a small, wizened figure with an overly large head.

He was dressed in a tunic, leggings, and leather boots, and he had a peaked cap on his head. He was grinning madly. A few feet from the wagon, both ghosts disappeared.

Cursing myself as a silly old man, I hauled out my handkerchief and wiped away tears of delight. My old Bessy was all right. More than all right. She appeared downright delighted with her new companion. I stuffed the hanky in my pocket and turned gruffly to Jacob. "What are you staring at?" I complained. "Come on! We've got ore to mine!"

Jacob chuckled and got back to work. Before joining him, I pulled out the pasty his missus had given me for lunch and broke off a large bite. I set it carefully next to the closest statue of a Tommy Knocker—which was a dead ringer for the little fellow riding my mule. "Thanks," I whispered softly. "Thanks."

And then I got on with my work.

20

Griffin

MERLIN

When I was growing up, there was a crazy old lady living on the outskirts of town who claimed she was the guardian of a vast buried treasure. Actually, she claimed that she was the guardian of the guardian, which was really weird. I mean, come on. Who in this day and age believes in mythical guardians?

Crazy Alice was the name we kids called her—when she wasn't around. The rudest ones said it to her face. She always wore long, flowing robes, and often she had a turban wrapped around her head. What with her deep-set black eyes and her long fingers, each bearing a ring with a different "magical" stone, she was quite a sight in our sleepy Oregon town.

According to the kids at school, the supposed guardian of the treasure was a massive, mythical being called a griffin. I had no idea what that was but didn't want to say so in front of my friends. So I looked it up in the school library. Turns out a griffin was a strange creature with the head, wings, and foreclaws of an eagle and the body, back legs, and tail of a lion. The dictionary said that griffins were considered to be majestic, since their bodies included both the king of the beasts and the king of the birds. The dictionary also confirmed that griffins were typically the guardians of treasure troves and went on to explain that they were considered a symbol of divine power. *Yikes*, I thought. So Crazy Alice is the guardian of the guardian of divine power? I shook my head and closed the thick volume thoughtfully.

My parents considered Crazy Alice harmless, though I was instructed not to bother her or go near her house. You know, parents really should know better than that. Any kid with pluck will tell you that such a restriction is guaranteed to produce the opposite result of that intended. So it should surprise no one that I instantly concocted a plan with Pete and Stanley—two of my best buddies—to sneak over to Crazy Alice's house one night to see if we could find the "treasure" or maybe even spot the griffin.

We had to wait until the weekend for our treasure hunt, since it had to happen on a day on which we could each reasonably "spend the night" with one another. That way, we could convince each of our parents that we were at one of the others' homes. It seemed to take forever for Saturday to come, but finally we were free and heading out on our adventure.

Crazy Alice lived on the edge of town in a log cabin on a high ridge surrounded by pines. It was a creepy place, even in the daylight, and not particularly well kept. The yard was full of tall grass and weeds. We rode our bikes through the darkened streets until we found ourselves on the windy side road leading to Crazy Alice's little cabin. The sky was perfectly clear and full of stars, but the wind was very chilly for a late spring evening, and we were all shivering as we peddled our bicycles, despite the exercise. Trust Crazy Alice to live on top of a steep ridge!

The moon slowly rose above the mountains and shone down brightly on the dark road where we peddled and peddled our way uphill. The moonlight made the going much easier, since there were no streetlights along this deserted stretch of road.

Before long, Stan started complaining bitterly about the cold and the climb. Stan was a plump kid who was more of a brain than a jock. I had known he'd find this ride hard, but he had insisted on coming. Stan had just convinced us to take a break when a shadow suddenly covered the moon. The wind whooshed around the top of the trees as if fanned by a huge pair of wings, and we heard a single sharp cry from above. All of us jumped, and Pete jerked his handlebars so hard he nearly crashed into a tree.

"What was that?" Stan shouted, his voice sounding hoarse and strained.

"I have no idea," I replied, looking up above the trees where the shadow had appeared. "Maybe a storm cloud?"

"Maybe a griffin?" Pete suggested, picking himself up off the ground and limping over to the place where I'd stopped my bike.

"There's no such thing as griffins," I scoffed. "Come on. We're nearly there."

Stan groaned loudly but followed Pete and I up the road to the little clearing among the pines where Crazy Alice's cabin stood at the top of the ridge. We tucked our bikes under some bushes and tiptoed silently toward the little house. There was a light on in the front window, but I was more interested in the softer, flickering light coming from a very low window in the back that looked like it led to the basement. After all, where else would you keep treasure?

Stan bumped into the axle of a crumbling wagon that stood by a gnarled apple tree in the center of the yard. Muffling his curses, he hopped on one foot, rubbing his shin and making terrible faces in the moonlight. Pete had already reached the small window in the back and was lying on his stomach to look inside. Ignoring Stan's complaints, I joined him.

At first I was disappointed. It looked like a perfectly ordinary cellar, with a washer–dryer combo, a cement floor, a clothesline strung next to the furnace, and lots of clutter. Then I noticed the little box sitting under a weak, flickering lightbulb. Several small creatures were mewling and crawling about inside it.

Stan dropped down beside us, whispering: "Are those kittens?"

"Must be," Pete said. But I wasn't so sure. There was something strange about the way they were walking. Their front feet seemed to work differently than their hind feet. Then one of the creatures raised its little head, and I saw fluff all over its face and a beak where its nose and mouth should be.

"Baby griffins," I gasped. And that's when we were attacked.

A whoosh of air slammed into us, and we heard a harsh scream and the flapping of enormous wings. I rolled over and saw a giant, winged shadow descending rapidly from the treetops. The moonlight glinted off huge talons poised to grab us.

"Run," I shouted, rolling upright. I dove toward the bushes where our bikes were hidden and heard pounding feet and gasping breaths as my friends raced after me. The flapping sound followed us as we leapt on our bikes and skidded out of the little yard and down the steep hill. Heart pounding madly, I peddled faster than I ever had in my life, adding as much speed as I could to the already-fast descent from the steep ridge.

"Duck," Pete screamed as a large shadow swooped low above us. We ducked, and I felt a stinging sensation on top of my head as sharp talons grazed my scalp.

GRIFFIN

The turn onto the main road was just ahead. I braked with all my might and skidded sharply into the turn, followed by Stan and Pete. The great shadow above us overshot the turn and kept flying toward the trees at the side of the road. The griffin screamed in rage and swerved upward to avoid crashing into a giant Douglas fir. Taking advantage of this, we rode as fast as we could toward town, dodging left onto this road and right onto another to shake our aerial pursuer.

After fifteen minutes of frantic biking, Pete shouted out that he thought we were in the clear. At once, we tumbled off our bikes onto someone's carefully manicured lawn—I had no idea whose it was and I didn't care—and tried desperately to catch our breath. My legs were shaking so badly from nerves and the strain of peddling that they wouldn't hold me up. I sank down into the soft grass and just lay there trembling from head to toe. Stan was in worse shape. He fell over without dismounting, lying in a tangle of aluminum taking huge gasping breaths. Pete had flopped facedown onto the grass and didn't even lift his head to breathe, though his nose was squashed into a dandelion.

"Do you think it's safe?" asked Pete when he got his breath back. He rolled over and looked at me. I squinted up at the sky. It was empty of everything save the moon and the gentle glow of the stars.

"I think so," I said cautiously. I got up onto my hands and knees and crawled over to disentangle poor Stan from his bike. He looked wiped out, and his plump figure was shaking all over. My knees wobbled a bit when I stood up, but not so much that I couldn't walk. I urged the others up, and we all walked our bikes the rest of the way home.

We crashed at Stan's house, which was the closest, and seriously overslept, which meant we had to explain to his parents why we were all there instead of "over at Pete's place," which was where Stan had told them we would be. Pete's real good at making up plausible tales, and he concocted some brilliant piece of fiction that almost convinced Stan's folks. At least enough that they didn't yell at Stan until we went home.

I most emphatically did not want to ride back on my bike, but it was nearly a mile home, so I straddled the bar like an old, old man and peddled home, trying to ignore my protesting thighs. As I turned onto my street, I heard my Mom shout something from the front lawn. She was staring up at the house as I pulled into the driveway. The porch roof hid whatever she was looking at from view. My father came running out as I propped up my bike by the garage and stood with his hands on his hips, his face tight with anger.

"Just come look what some crazy person has done to our house!" Mom called to me.

My eyes widened in sudden fear as I recalled the huge shadow that had chased us down the ridge from Crazy Alice's. Forgetting my aches and pains, I bolted across the lawn to see what was wrong. Both my parents were glaring in anger at the second story. I looked up too, following their gaze. Six long gashes were scraped into the wood of the roof in two pairs of three. It looked as if giant bird claws had scraped their way across the house in the middle of the night. I took one look and fainted.

Mom and Dad were rather surprised by my reaction and hastened to tell me that they would "call the police" and make sure that the "crazy man" wouldn't come back. Not wanting to get into trouble—and frankly, because I figured they wouldn't believe me anyway—I didn't say a word about the previous night's escapade.

I found out later that both Stan and Pete's houses also bore the marks of an angry griffin, and we knew we'd had a lucky escape. The three of us vowed never to set foot on Crazy Alice's property again, and we never did.

The Cheshire Cat

EUGENE

Sarah knew as soon as she set foot on campus that something was very wrong. Amid all the hustle and bustle of life as a new freshman, she sensed a dark presence around the edge of the activity. A presence that silently harassed people who stood for light and goodness—and encouraging those who embraced the dark.

She didn't speak about what she sensed. She never had, since childhood. That was not her way, or the way of her people. She came from a long line of white wizards. From the farthest reaches of memory her ancestors had used herbs and faith healing and forces some would call magic to influence the world for the good. Everyone in her family had this ability, and Sarah was the strongest of her generation. Indeed, of many generations.

Sarah had chosen this particular university because it had a fabulous track and field program and was once the training place for the international track star Steve Prefontaine. Sarah herself was a skilled runner and was given a scholarship and a place on the track team. She was also majoring in premed, for Sarah was determined to be a certified physician as well as a white-magic healer.

As always seemed to happen, Sarah began collecting people around her with similar abilities, those who she sensed were exceptional towers of light in a dark world. There was a junior girl named Jessica who was a psychic, and a cute sophomore runner named Kenny who had the strongest ESP she'd ever encountered outside her family. There was Lisa, a freshman who lived in a haunted house and was able to see ghosts. And finally, there were twin brothers, Billy and Brett—both freshman runners—whose father was a Native American shaman and who both evidenced talent in herbs and natural medicine. Somehow, the six of them naturally came together over the first two months at university, eventually spending all their time together, enjoying one another's company, and quietly doing good.

It was Jessie who warned them about the Cheshire Cat. "He's been around as long as I've been here," she told them quietly one evening as they sprawled in their favorite corner in the student lounge, studying. "And the rumors say he's been in this part of the county even longer than there's been a city."

Sarah nodded gravely. She had quietly been investigating the source of darkness in her spare moments, and Jessie's information coincided with what she had learned elsewhere. She exchanged glances with fair-haired, blue-eyed Kenny, who gave her a shy smile and a nod. Sarah had known instantly upon meeting him—in one of those flashes that came to her out of the blue—that she would marry Kenny someday. They were a perfect fit. She smiled back and then turned to Jessie, questioning her closely about the rumors. Sarah was the unacknowledged leader of their group, and when she took an interest in something, they all did. Soon, everyone was gathering information about the Cheshire Cat.

He was a lord of darkness, Lisa told them after dinner the next week, after interviewing the ghost who haunted the university grounds. A high-ranking one, said the twins, who had gone home for the weekend and spent much of it conferring with their father. And completely evil. Kenny confirmed that the Cheshire Cat seemed to figure into most of the negative goings-on around the campus—fights, drugs, rebellion against authority. He was said to appear when people were at the tipping point of doing something wrong, and encourage them to jump over the edge. But whenever students tried to point people to the dark man who had guided them into trouble, he was never there.

"Have you ever seen him?" Sarah asked Kenny. He nodded and shuddered. "Just once," he said softly. "Waiting outside the track to talk to one of the runners after a particularly difficult meet last year. He was a tall, blond man with dark eyes and something about him that felt menacing. He ignored me completely and spent several minutes speaking to the other fellow. The next week, the runner was found to be taking drugs and was thrown off the team."

"So," Sarah said finally to the group of white wizards sitting around her in the student lounge. "What do we do about it?"

"Do?" asked a deep, lazy voice from just outside the circle. "Why should you do anything? What have I done to you?"

They all turned, startled by the new voice, and stared. A tall man who looked old enough to be a professor stood looking down at them with a mocking smile on his handsome face. Just as Kenny had described, he was a blond man with dark eyes and a handsome form. But to Sarah's trained eye, he seemed hazy about the edges, as if he stood in immense heat that made the air wobble around him. She could tell that Lisa and the twins

148

were right: he was an immensely powerful lord of the darkness. Not *the* dark lord, but one who was close to him.

Sarah looked straight into his dark eyes with the glint of red in them. She could feel him pushing at their little circle, sending waves of fear and shock and pain into their minds. Jessie was crying a little, tears running down her cheeks in spite of her efforts to control them. The twins were holding up medicine bags and chanting softly. Lisa was noticeably sweating in her effort to fight against the menacing voice sucking at her mind.

Only Kenny and Sarah seemed unaffected by the visitor's presence, and their appearance of unconcern was effected only by immense effort of will. Kenny held out his hand and Sarah took it. The immediate influx of power and support from this joining unlocked her voice. "Go away," she said, each syllable taut with power.

And the Cheshire Cat vanished, laughing.

There was a moment of profound silence. Then everyone sighed in relief. "Good lord," Billy cried, speaking for them all. "How do we get rid of that?"

"First we ward the campus," Sarah said slowly, powerful words from one of the ancient books of Moses already gleaming in her mind. "And then we banish him from Eugene. Forever, if possible. Or at least for this generation. Listen!"

They leaned close to one another, and Kenny quietly put a "don't listen" spell around the group so no one could overhear their plans. It was a complicated solution that Sarah proposed, and one she had never done herself, though she had been an observer at a banishing performed by her immensely stern and powerful grandfather.

The student wizards split up almost immediately and spent the next several days gathering materials, studying and sharing ancient spells and rituals, and trying to squeeze in time for homework and track practice in between. Lisa, Jessie, and the twins would be the primary spellcasters for the campus warding, and Kenny and Sarah would perform the banishing. The twins had located a node of power underneath one of the older building on campus, and they found a disused classroom within it and set up both spells there.

At midnight on Saturday, the wizards stood in place around the magic circle Kenny had drawn on the floor. They held hands and recited the words of the spell used to raise wards around the campus. As soon as the first syllable was spoken, Sarah felt the winds of change rising around them, catching at their clothes and blowing their hair. Around her neck, the amulet of power that had been passed down in her family since the days of Moses began to glow as the twins called upon the powers of light to raise wards of protection over their campus, and Jessie and Lisa asked the angels of light to cast out the darkness already within. It was a strong spell and well cast.

For a moment, when they finished speaking, there was silence. Then a massive surge of power, both akin to and nothing like a surge of white light exploded forth from their magic circle. Sarah felt it sweeping across campus and heard invisible, dark entities wailing as they were driven before it. Even Lisa's favorite ghost was affected. For a moment, Sarah had a vision of it holding tightly to the overhanging branches of a tree as the power tore at it like the winds of a tornado. Then the wards were up, and all around them the mental atmosphere of the campus lightened, as if everyone within had breathed a sigh of relief.

Better, Sarah thought. Much better. She nodded to Kenny, whose skill in teleportation was even stronger than her own. Suddenly, the two of them were outside campus, outside the wards, standing at the crossroads. And there, as if summoned, stood the Cheshire Cat, looking very displeased.

"I knew you were trouble. I told the boss we should be rid of you as soon as you set foot on campus. This is my place!"

As the wicked blond man spoke, he waved one hand, and a group of massively built thugs ran into the crossroads from behind the parked cars where they had crouched out of sight. Sarah quickly raised a shield, which knocked most of the men backward onto the ground, but one of them had thrown a rock that smashed the side of Kenny's head before the shield spell took hold. He fell to the pavement, blood flowing from his temple. With a cry of anger and fear, Sarah dropped to her knees beside him, while outside the shield the thugs jeered and the Cheshire Cat stood silently, watching with a smile.

"I'm okay," Kenny reassured her, clapping a hand to his head. *He most assuredly was not*, Sarah thought, her hands trembling. But she saw that he was in no immediate danger. "Go on. Finish it, Sarah," he said, touching her cheek with his free hand. "I know you can." She drew a deep breath that sounded more like a gasp, nodded to Kenny, and stood to face the Cheshire Cat. Around her neck, the amulet started to glow.

"You belong to this place no longer, son of evil. I banish you in the Name of Names that cannot be uttered by mortal man," Sarah said, using the ritual words she had once heard her powerful grandfather speak to another such evil demon long ago. She went on calmly, speaking words of power, words of light that came to her mind from the ancient spellbooks of

THE CHESHIRE CAT

Moses. Behind her, she felt Kenny pouring his strength into her. Outside, the thugs cowered, some fleeing from her as she began to glow from within, power surging out from her toward the Cheshire Cat.

She could feel him pushing back at her, still calm and sardonic. Around them, all the streetlights went dark, and the glimmer of lights from the city darkened. The wind picked up again. Not the winds of change that accompanied strong magic, but the winds of death and despair that came from Hell itself. With them came dark shadows, thin wraiths, and broad banshees, horrible twisting nightmares full of sharp teeth and rustling wings. The silent roar became deafening, and the rest of the thugs fled before the roiling darkness that came pressing in on the shield that Kenny struggled to maintain while Sarah cast her spell.

Sarah staggered under the weight of the dark magic pouring from the Cheshire Cat. Her knees were buckling. Underfoot, the pavement was growing hotter and hotter, as if the searing lava pits of Hell were bubbling to the surface. The road burned red, and only the fragile shield spell kept Sarah and Kenny from burning with it. But Sarah sensed that the spell could not last much longer against the power pouring forth from the Cheshire Cat. His blond hair writhed in the terrible, death-filled wind, and his arms spread wide as he summoned all the evil powers at his command. Sarah knew she was out of time. The shield would fail before she could finish her banishment spell, and she and Kenny would die, right here at the crossroads.

Sarah gasped desperately as the weight of evil bore down on her, until she was barely able to continue speaking the words of the spell. Every nasty thought she had ever had crowded into her mind, shaming her and diluting her concentration. Sarah fought to clear her mind, speaking from a throat so dry she could barely stammer. The heat from the pavement was making her face and arms go red and her head spin. She could hear Kenny whimper as he poured power into her at the cost of his own personal defenses.

Then there came a clap of displaced air. Suddenly Lisa, Jessie, and the twins were with them, flowing power into the shield and into Sarah and Kenny. The terrible heat abated, and the howling, swirling darkness drew away. Sarah stood straighter, her voice becoming clearer and firmer, her will suddenly strong. She felt the winds of change rising inside the shield, and outside it too, driving away the demons of darkness. The pavement outside cooled, and the fires burned low and then died away, until nothing was left but the Cheshire Cat, facing them with a stern face, too proud to look away from them even as he was being banished from his chosen territory. The amulet around Sarah's neck flashed once, twice, three times. Sarah called out the long syllables of the Cheshire Cat's true name, each one burning her throat as she spoke it, using it to bind and banish him. There came a flash of lightning and a clap of thunder. And the Cheshire Cat was gone.

The winds died down, and Sarah's knees gave way. She collapsed to the ground beside the bleeding Kenny as the shield spell faded. The two of them clung together as Jessie, Lisa, and the twins crowded around them.

Sarah pushed them away at last, her hair bloody where it had brushed Kenny's temple. "How did you get here?" she asked her friends. "How did you know?"

"We felt your spell becoming unbalanced," Brett said. "And we knew you needed help."

"And you aren't the only ones who know how to trans-locate!" his twin added with a grin.

"Thanks!" Kenny said gratefully. Holding tightly to one another, he and Sarah helped each other to their feet. "We owe you one."

Brett smiled mischievously. "We know," he said.

"Do you think he's gone for good?" asked Jessica, glancing nervously around as one by one, the streetlamps flickered back to life.

Sarah reached out with her mind, sensing the life around them, sensing the campus wards, sensing the level of the banishment she had imposed upon the Cheshire Cat with the help of her friends.

"I think so," she said at last. "For this generation, at least. And maybe for the next."

"A job well done," Kenny pronounced, waving a bloody hand for emphasis. "Now, I don't know about the rest of you, but I could use some sleep. I've got an exam tomorrow!"

At least they had survived to take their exams, Sarah thought, leaning into Kenny's shoulder as they walked back toward the warded campus, arms twined tightly together.

Behind her, a puddle of oil that had dripped from one of the parked cars formed slowly into the shape of a face with burning, dark eyes full of hatred. The Cheshire Cat watched the students return to their campus, grinding his teeth as they passed through the wards and out of sight. The binding spell that held him was not strong enough to keep him forever. He had the advantage of time, and he could afford to wait.

22

Bandage Man

CANNON BEACH

My dog Tinker and I had been hiking and camping our way up the Oregon coast most of the summer. I was done with college at last and due to start work at a big company in Portland come the fall. I'd promised myself one summer of freedom before starting the nine-to-five grind, and this was it. I'd spent a lot of time fishing on the Rogue before making my way slowly north. I planned to wander all the way to Astoria and do some fishing on the Columbia River before I went back to Portland to find an apartment and settle into adult life.

I was thinking about my new job, and Tinker was barking and chasing his tail happily as I set up my tent for the night at one of the local RV parks. It was the tail end of the season, and there weren't many guests at the park. I had the tenting area all to myself, which suited me fine. I was a bit of a free spirit, and I liked my solitude, and the thought of my soon-to-come desk job depressed me. So I changed into jogging shorts, grabbed Tinker's leash, and headed southward, down the beach toward Haystack Rock. As luck would have it, the tide was going out and we got a good, close-up view of the world's third-tallest sea stack. It was a massive affair and worth seeing.

I took a quick dip in the ocean—cold!—and headed back to my tent to change for dinner. I figured I'd go into Cannon Beach for a bite. I left poor Tinker tied to a tree near my tent, whining and barking indignantly at being left behind, and ambled my way slowly back toward town, choosing to walk rather than take the free shuttle bus they offered at the campground. It was such a gorgeous evening that a stroll seemed in order, and I was happy to be free and on my own, rather than trapped in a stuffy office.

I found a bar in town and settled down to eat a very good hamburger and listen to the locals talking. The talk was mostly of sports and fishing. But as it grew dark outside, the conversation turned to a fairly recent sighting of someone the locals called the "Bandage Man." I perked up my ears. This sounded interesting. Apparently, some high school kids had taken a six-pack to the local dump this past spring and had sat drinking in the back of a pickup truck before a high school basketball game. Suddenly, they heard a sound in the woods surrounding the place and saw a flash of white as a massive figure wrapped head to toe in bandages came toward them, arms outstretched. The kids did what anyone would have done in the circumstances. They crowded into the cab of the pickup and drove off in a spurt of dirt and gravel. The huge "mummy" leapt into the back of the truck as it drove past and thumped at the window until the glass broke and shattered. The kids drove like crazy toward town, and the figure finally leapt off the speeding truck as it reached town limits. The shaken students had to be treated for cuts from the glass but were otherwise unharmed. The story had been much discussed in town ever since.

When the talk turned to other things, I moseyed up to the bar for another beer and asked the bartender about it.

He chuckled a bit in a "don't believe everything you hear" manner and told me that the Bandage Man was a local legend. Apparently a doctor and his wife had been driving in the vicinity a number of years back, and their car had been totaled in an accident. When the police arrived, they found the doctor's wife in the wreckage, but not the doctor himself. A massive man well over six feet tall, he would have been a hard figure to miss. The police thought he might have lost his wits in the accident and wandered off, but he was never found. However, it wasn't long after the accident that the mummy the locals referred to as the "Bandage Man" began making his appearance. Every few years, a new story would pop up. He was said to have destroyed property, hidden in the back of parked cars or pickup trucks and attacked their drivers, and once, even grabbed a hitchhiker right off the road and carted him away over his bandaged shoulder. Others believed that he ate the local dogs.

"Sounds like a nasty character," I remarked.

"He makes a good campfire story," the bartender said with a grin. "I always got a good snuggle out of my wife after telling her a Bandage Man story!"

I laughed, paid my tab, and headed back to camp.

That was the last chuckle I had that evening. When I got back to the tent, Tinker was missing, leash and all. I spent the rest of the evening searching for him, questioning both my fellow campers and the staff of the RV park. No one had seen him.

"He'll probably show up in the morning," the desk attendant said soothingly, and I hoped she was right. Tinker was usually obedient, and I couldn't see him trying to run off. Unless the leash came untied and he followed me to town, I thought as I undressed and crawled into my sleeping bag. If so, he'd get my scent and follow it back here.

Comforted by the thought, I sank into an uneasy sleep.

I was awakened in the night by the sound of footsteps approaching my tent through the trees. Suddenly, the sparsely occupied RV park and my solitary space therein didn't seem so nice, especially with my dog missing. *Don't be stupid*, I thought, lying very still in my sleeping bag. *It's probably a night watchman. Or a cougar, or a bear*, my treacherous thoughts whispered. *Or maybe even the Bandage Man!* I cursed my vivid imagination and stayed still.

A foul smell of decaying flesh and dead, rotting leaves suddenly filled the tent. My mouth went dry as I saw a dark shape silhouetted against the nylon roof, outlined by the glow of a half-moon overhead. And then a massive fist punched downward, stretching the nylon, and the towering shape gave a wordless roar. Heart pounding, I screamed in terror, fighting my way desperately out of the sleeping bag trapping my legs. A second massive punch ripped the nylon, and I caught a glimpse of dirty white bandages through the tear. The zipper of the sleeping bag was stuck. I ripped it open, squirmed out like a snake, and fumbled with the zipper of the tent as the massive fist smashed against the roof for the third time. The tent collapsed around me as I leapt out the door and ran for my life down the road toward the main buildings and safety. Footsteps pounded behind me, and I felt a whoosh of air as if rotting arms had tried to grab me from behind. I ducked and a loose, rotting bandage slapped the top of my head. Dodging to the right, I raced as fast as I could toward the closest streetlamp illuminating the grounds. I heard my pursuer slow and crash off into the woods.

BANDAGE MAN

I kept running until I reached the office. It was closed. I spent the rest of the night huddled with my back against the wall, staring frantically around me until the sky lightened toward sunrise.

I waited until the day-staff arrived and then reported the incident. I didn't mention the rotten smell or the bandages. I just said that someone had attacked my tent in the middle of the night and that I had remained by the office, fearing to return to my tent alone. The man running the office was very kind. He accompanied me back to my campsite, never remarking upon my shaking hands or pale face. As we approached, I saw, here and there, bits of rotting white bandages strewn along the road. The office attendant saw them too, and his eyes widened. Then we reached my campsite and stared in horror at the damage. The tent and sleeping bag were ripped to pieces, my clothes were scattered everywhere, and the half-eaten body of my dog Tinker lay on top of the picnic table, strewn with rotten bandages.

I retched, threw up what was left of last night's dinner, and ran back toward the office, the attendant right behind me. I reported the incident to the police, recovered my wallet and a few belongings from the wreckage, and headed back to Portland, devastated by the loss of my dog and too scared even to think about finishing my trip. Suddenly, a boring desk job sounded just fine by me.

It was years before I took another camping vacation, and I never set foot in Cannon Beach again.

23

Laughing Devil

GOLD BEACH

'Round about 1850 or so, a grandpa and his boy living in the Willamette Valley heard from a passing tradesman that gold had been found in the hills along the Rogue River. Gold fever hit them two bachelors within minutes of hearing the report, and they decided they'd best get in a claim lickety-split before any of them forty-niners down in Cally-fornia heard about it. They hightailed it to the coast and went straight to the closest general store to stock up on food and placer mining supplies. Cost them a mint, but they didn't care. Soon they'd be rich!

While they were at the store, the owner came out of the back to chat with the new prospectors. During the visit, he warned them to avoid Laughing Devil Canyon. It was said to be haunted by an evil spirit that twisted the heads off anyone roaming through the canyon after dark, dragging their bodies up to its lair and gnawing on their bones.

The prospectors burst out laughing when they heard this load of hokum. A laughing devil! What was a devil or two when gold was on the line? The storekeeper shook his head and handed them their parcels. He'd warned them. That was all he could do.

"What say we jog on up to Laughing Devil Canyon tonight, partner?" said the grizzle-haired, red-faced prospector to his grandson, who he'd raised as his own son after his daughter and her husband died in a fire.

"Sure thing, Pa!" said the curly-haired imp. "Betcha that story was put out by a gold miner who didn't want anyone stealing his claim!"

"Bet yer right," said his grandpa.

Chuckling happily, the old man and the young boy stomped out into the hills, keeping their eyes open for any promising sparkles in the streams or interesting-looking seams in the jutting rocks. They'd obtained directions to Laughing Devil Canyon from the lady who ran the post office, and they headed straight there.

It was about noon when they entered the narrow canyon and started making their way through the dim light that filtered down from the high walls above.

"Gloomy," said the boy cheerfully. "Makes a body think there might be somethin' in that Devil story after all!"

"'Bout a million dollars in gold, I'm thinkin'," said his grandpa. "Jest you keep prospecting!"

Slowly, the boy and his grandpa made their way through the deep gulch, searching the walls and streambed for tell-tale signs of gold.

Round about dusk, the boy let out a yelp of excitement and started shouting for his grandpa. "I've found it! I've found me some gold!"

The old man came a-running, his red face glowing almost as bright as the setting sun. Man and boy started panning in the stream, and gee-whilikers if they didn't find a mess of gold right then and there!

"We got ourselves a claim!" shouted Grandpa, tearing off his hat and throwing it in the air.

"Gold!" shouted the boy. "Gold!"

They danced around in the streambed, throwing water into the air for sheer joy.

And that's when the laughter began. It started low; just an evil-sounding chuckle that raised the hair on the back of the neck and froze the limbs in place. The miners stared at one another, droplets of water falling all around them, as the laughter got louder and louder, bouncing off the walls of the narrow gulch. It didn't sound human. It had strange undertones that made the whole body shiver and shake and set the feet to running before the mind could register the movement.

Abandoning packs, gold, and reason, the boy and his grandpa raced out of the stream and down the length of the gulch as the laughter grew louder and louder, hurting their ears and making tears of pain sting their eyes. Darkness was falling swiftly around them as they stumbled over rocks and jumped fallen trees in sheer panic.

Then the boy let out a scream of terror and started backpedaling as a huge, winged shape shot over his head and landed right in front of him, blocking the path through the narrow canyon. It was a foul creature, more skeleton than living flesh. It towered ten feet above them, and it had giant leathery wings like a bat and a narrow, evil face like a crocodile, with the same sharp teeth.

Grandpa ground to a halt behind the boy and grabbed hold of his shoulders, trying to stay upright. The two ended up in a heap at the feet of the Laughing Devil, and the beast started chuckling again in the same horrible, rumbling tone that made

LAUGHING DEVIL

their bones vibrate with terror. Reaching down casually with one claw, it ripped the head right off the struggling boy and ate it in one bite. His Grandpa gave a scream of rage as his grandson's blood spilled out all over his head and body. He launched himself at the creature, batting at it fiercely with his fists. The Laughing Devil grabbed him with both claws and ripped him cleanly in two. Blood and guts spilled all over the ground, soiling the headless body of the boy. The Laughing Devil chuckled again, its laughter getting louder and louder as darkness encompassed the canyon. It wrapped its tail around the boy's body and leapt into the air, carrying the corpses up and up to its den, hot blood dripping onto the earth far below.

The next morning, the storekeeper and two of his employees came to the Laughing Devil Canyon and walked upstream until they found the prospectors' packs and mining gear. Quietly, they packed everything up and carted it down the canyon and back to town to sell to the next greedy fool who passed that way. The last man in line carefully kicked sand over the blood on the ground and made sure the fake gold deposits were back in place. Then he hurried after the storekeeper, grinning to himself as he ran. The boss was right, as usual. Greenhorns always came to the canyon to pan for gold, in spite of their warnings. They were making a fortune off this place!

Up in its aerie on top of the canyon wall, the Laughing Devil burped contentedly. Pulling another bone off its pile, it started to gnaw.

24

The Devil's Sink

My family moved from Portland to the Elgin in 1910 to help my grandma run the family ranch after my grandpa had passed away. Pa'd grown up on the ranch and was glad to be back home again, rounding up cattle and raising horses. He was a cowboy at heart and happily gave up his desk job for ranching. He always said he'd never make a fortune, but it was the only life for him!

I was a boy of ten at the time, and I loved my new home. When I wasn't doing chores, I was learning to ride and rope and wrangle. Real cowboy stuff. I wanted to learn to ride a bull too, but Pa said I had to wait until I was older. But Pa showed me how to pan for gold in the local streams that drained into the Grand Ronde River. Gold was a big thing in the Wallowa Mountains. Folks liked to discuss the mysterious Nez Perce mine that was the secret source of the tribe's wealth. And the townsfolk claimed there was another lost mine up by the Devil's Sink.

I was intrigued by the name of the place. What *was* the Devil's Sink? When I asked Pa, he told me it was a place where the basalt rock formations laid down by ancient volcanoes had collapsed into themselves, forming "sinks" that filled with water and became lakes. It was a rugged area full of lava extrusions and cracks and crevices. A mysterious place that the local tribes claimed was haunted by evil spirits.

I was fascinated by the notion of the Devil's Sink and eager to visit it, especially after I heard about the lost treasure from the neighbor boys about my age. The story of the treasure was pretty simple. Sometime in the 1850s, shortly after gold was discovered in "them thar hills" of Oregon, a couple of fellows driving a freight wagon from Boise to Walla Walla found their path blocked by a huge fallen log just outside Elgin. One of the drivers jumped down to move the tree and was shot in the heart by a band of masked desperados. The bandits surrounded the wagon and ordered the one remaining driver to put his hands up and step down, which he did. Meanwhile, the thieves rummaged in the back of the wagon—and struck gold. Literally. Among the supplies was a small chest that was found to contain about $60,000 in gold coins. The bandits loaded the coins into their saddlebags along with a host of other goods. Then they sent the frightened driver on his way while they rode off toward Devil's Sink, where they had their camp.

The sheriff was summoned by the freight driver as soon as he reached the next town, and he rode with a posse of men to the Devil's Sink. There, a terrific gun-battle ensued, leaving every bandit dead but one young fellow who lay clinging feebly to life as the sheriff and his men searched in vain for the saddlebags full of gold. The sheriff took the desperado to the local doctor, hoping he'd fix the lad up so that he could be interrogated. But the boy had lost too much blood, and he died. Everyone thought that was the end of it until the pretty nurse who worked at the doctor's surgery came forward, claiming the desperado had confessed to her on his deathbed that the saddlebags full of gold had been dropped into the Big Sink, the larger of the two lakes, when the thieves heard the posse approaching.

The sheriff and his men went back to the lake and prodded about with long sticks, while the lone swimmer in the group dove beneath the water trying to locate the gold. It was no good. The swimmer declared that Big Sink was "bottomless," and the treasure was abandoned.

Of course, many treasure hunters visited the sink after that, trying their hand at diving for gold. But no one ever found it, and many concluded that the Devil's Sink was indeed bottomless. A few folks also claimed that evil spirits had accosted them while they were out in the middle of the lake. The townsfolk just laughed when they heard such stories. Why, the treasure hunters must have been drinking a little too much applejack!

Well, no one may have found the treasure yet, but that didn't stop me from deciding to try. First chance I got, I saddled my pony and packed my saddlebags full of Ma's garden trowels and the snorkel and mask I'd ordered from a catalog. Of course, I didn't tell Ma and Pa why I needed snorkeling supplies. They thought I wanted to explore the duck pond and the streams around the ranch.

I enjoyed the long ride through the hills and canyons surrounding my new home, and I stopped once around noon to enjoy the bread and cheese Ma had packed for my lunch. The mountains around me were so beautiful it sometimes made my throat ache and my eyes sting to look at them, and I had to hum loudly to myself to keep from bawling my eyes out like a sissy.

My pulse started pounding in excitement when I came 'round a bend in the trail and spotted Big Sink ahead of me. I was nearly there! Treasure awaited. Imagine what I could buy with $60,000 in gold coins!

My pony shifted uneasily under me as we moved down the trail toward the lake. His muscles bunched up like he wanted to rear, and it took all my new-learned skills at riding to keep him on course. A coldish wind had sprung up, too, blowing around us. There was a strange whistling, hissing sound in the wind, almost as if the far-off voices of the dead were whispering a warning. I shivered at the thought and then laughed at my foolishness. I was letting some old Indian legend scare me.

I spurred on my reluctant pony, and we walked on until we reached a nice flat spot. Then I tied Trigger's reins around an outcropping and stripped down to my shorts and an old ragged pair of shoes I'd rescued from the dustbin. Thrusting my clothes into the saddlebag, I took out my snorkeling gear and a garden trowel and waded out into the water, shivering as the cold wind whipped around me, whistling in my ears. I sank down into the chilly waters of the sink and started swimming along the bottom, digging with the trowel. I stuck to the shallow spots, breathing through the snorkel as I swam this way and that. I found nothing.

Finally, I surfaced and threw the snorkel on the rocks by the shore, since I needed to dive deeper than the air tube would reach. Then I slipped back under water and continued down into the murky depths toward the center of the Devil's Sink, peering at the weeds and silt through my mask and trying not to think of monsters and giant fish coming to grab me. My breath gave out quickly, and I surfaced amid all the silt my trowel had raised from the bottom.

THE DEVIL'S SINK

This is not going well, I thought, glancing over at Trigger. He was shifting uneasily, and I caught a flash of white as he rolled his eyes and shied as far back from the water as his bridle would allow. The hissing, mumbling sound was back again, much louder now. It seemed to echo around the lake as I drew in a deep breath, preparing to make another dive. The sun had gone behind a dark bank of clouds, and the wind was worse than ever. Mist was rising along the edges of the sink, and the shadows had darkened until a strange twilight lay over everything. I let out my breath and tread water, suddenly spooked by the realization that I was alone in this strange, wild spot with a storm coming. One more dive, I told myself, and then Trigger and I were done.

I sank below the surface. The water seemed much darker and colder with the sun behind the clouds. I could barely see at all by the time I was three feet down. I flailed about with the trowel blindly, and felt something resist. I put down my free hand and touched a slimy, leathery surface. I clutched at it, my lungs aching, and kicked my way up to the surface. I gasped for breath as soon as my head was out of the water and then held up the bit of leather I'd found. It was hard to see in the storm-induced twilight. On shore, Trigger whinnied suddenly, a sound of fear, but I ignored it, heart pounding as I realized I held a decaying bit of saddlebag.

Suddenly, the waters of the lake were lit by a greenish glow that grew brighter and brighter with each passing second. I looked up, startled. Through my dripping mask, I saw writhing green figures with pitiless black eyes, long, clawed arms, and bodies bloated out of all semblance of human shape floating just above the surface of the lake. They surrounded me, and I knew without a doubt that these were the evil spirits that had frightened the native tribesmen for years. I screamed in terror at the sight of the devilish faces, as gust upon gust of a rotten stench flowed over me. I swam for my life toward shore through the only gap I saw in the ring of glowing green spirits, dropping the trowel but holding tightly to the bit of leather saddlebag.

I have no idea if I was pursued. I didn't look back. I just staggered ashore, ran to untie my rearing pony, and leapt on his back without even removing the snorkeling mask. Trigger and I were up and out of that terrible, creepy place in a matter of minutes and well away from the lake by the time the massive storm roared down upon us with brilliant flashes of lightning and claps of thunder. Knowing it wasn't safe to stay out in the open, I scouted around through the downpour until I found a small cave within one of the strange outcroppings of rock. Trigger and I both huddled inside it, still trembling in terror.

I was dripping wet, covered with mud, and shaking with fear and cold. Even the bit of saddlebag I clutched didn't comfort me. Slowly, I removed a towel from my pack and dried my wet skin. Shrugging out of my shorts, I pulled fresh clothes on and thrust the rotting bit of leather and my soaking swim gear and mask back into the pack. My snorkel was back on the shores of the Devil's Sink, and there it would remain.

Dry now, but still clammy-skinned and cold, I leaned back against the stone inside the mouth of the cave and idly played with some quartz rocks lying on the ground. Outside, the rain pounded down, and the lightning made a spectacular show in the sky. To my surprise, Trigger stayed calm during the thunderstorm, in spite of the loud thunderclaps and bright lightning. After the devils we'd seen by the sink, nothing as mild as a summer storm could frighten my pony.

When the storm passed, I stood up and tucked four or five of the prettiest quartz rocks I'd found into the saddlebags to give to my Ma. Then I rode out on Trigger, looking over the rain-washed scenery in a bit of a panic, since I hadn't taken my bearings when we left the Devil's Sink. I couldn't see the sun behind the clouds, so I took a guess and turned left out of the cave. I was wrong. Trigger and I wandered about for hours until the clouds passed and we could take a measure from the sun as it lowered behind the mountains to the west. We finally found our way down to the river, and from there back home. It was full dark when we arrived at the barn. Pa and Ma saw us ride into the yard and rushed out to yell at me.

I knew I'd get into trouble for my escapade, but I was so frightened by what had happened that I had to tell them about it. As I unsaddled Trigger and brushed him down, I related the story to my parents. When I told them I'd ridden out to the Devil's Sink by myself, my Pa leapt up from the hay bale on which he'd been sitting, and his face turned bright red with anger. "You did what?" he shouted, startling the horses in the barn. Ma hushed him. "He obviously got back safe and sound, dear. Let Davy get on with the story."

Pa's face turned redder still when he found out I'd been snorkeling all alone in the sink, but he grew thoughtful when I gasped out the part about the dead voices on the wind and the glowing green spirits I'd seen. He nodded several times. Pa had heard all about the evil spirits from a Native American friend of his, but he hadn't believed in them until now.

"I ought to tan your hide for pulling such a prank," Pa said when I finished my story. "But I think the ghosts already did it for me. You won't be pulling another such stunt anytime soon, I'm thinking."

I shook my head frantically, my whole body shaking at the thought of going near the Devil's Sink again. I put the brush and curry comb away with trembling hands as Pa picked up my packs.

"Well, let's see that piece of saddlebag you found," said Pa. He opened the bag and started pulling out the wet clothes and quartz rocks and put them on the bale of hay beside Ma. Then he picked up the rotting leather and turned it this way and that, examining it closely. Beside him, Ma exclaimed over the pretty rocks and held them up in the lamplight, studying them as carefully as Pa studied the piece of leather.

"Frankly, I'm not convinced this was the desperado's saddlebag," Pa said finally. "Anyone could have thrown it into the sink. Did you see any gold coins while you were down there?"

I shook my head.

"Davy," Ma said at this juncture, a strange note in her voice. "Where'd you get these pieces of quartz?"

"They were lying on the floor of the cave where Trigger and I sheltered from the storm," I said, leaning against the door of the stall and looking at her curiously.

"Do you know where that cave is? Can you find it again?" Ma asked.

I shrugged. "I don't know," I said. "We got pretty lost riding away from the Devil's Sink. Why?"

Ma answered by pointing to a very large gold nugget caught inside one of the rocks. I gaped at it with my mouth wide open.

Pa exclaimed and took the rock gently from her hand. "Gold," he whispered softly. "You found gold."

All the rocks had gold in and on them. We exclaimed over the find and then hurried into the house, where Pa pulled out a map and I attempted to retrace my steps to the cave where I'd found the gold-bearing quartz.

We spent the best part of the next month searching the hills and canyons from our ranch to the Devil's Sink, looking for the cave where I sheltered from the storm. But we never found it. In the end, the only things I had to show for my escapade were a rotting piece of saddlebag, and five gold-bearing rocks.

Oh well. If it came right down to it, I'd rather be a cowboy than a rich man, anyway.

#

25

I sank down gratefully on the wooden bench just inside the fort and leaned back against the hewn-log wall behind me with a sigh of relief. I looked around, taking in the replica of Fort Clatsop in which I found myself. My first impression was that it was a very small fort—much smaller than I'd expected from the size of the Corps of Discovery, the group of explorers led by the famous Meriwether Lewis and William Clark. But this was supposed to be an accurate reproduction of the group's winter camp, so I supposed it must have been this tiny. Really, it was nothing more than a wide aisle between two long, low buildings, each containing a few doors and small windows. The whole fort was surrounded by a tall fence made of sharp, pointed logs, and there were a few small chimney openings on the roof to let out the smoke from the rough fireplaces inside.

The warm sun felt good as it caressed my head and face. I closed my eyes and sighed, wishing the nagging pain in my arm would go away. I heard my bride of three months, Marie, talking to a park staffer as she wandered happily in and out of the various buildings and rooms, carefully reconstructed to represent fort life as it had been in 1806. I was an avid history buff myself, but at the moment I couldn't care less about the exhibit. I hadn't slept well the previous night. I kept waking up with a feeling that something was wrong at home. And today my arm and shoulder were hurting off and on. I'd tried ringing my folks back east, but no one answered. No one was home at my brother's place, either. My gut told me something was wrong. But until I was able to talk to someone, I wasn't going to panic.

Marie knew better than to ignore my "hunches"—really, presentiments, plain and simple. I'd had them since childhood. When I was in second grade, for example, I woke up in the middle of the night smelling smoke and hearing firemen's voices as they worked the water hoses. I'd panicked the whole family with my screams, and it wasn't until I'd roused the house that I realized the fire was at my elementary school. Nobody believed me until the school called the next morning to tell us that classes were suspended until they could find a new building for us.

In middle school, I went into a trance right in the middle of a walking tour at Gettysburg, and no one could get me to move or speak for five minutes. During those five minutes, it seemed to me that I had walked into a horrendous battle full of suffocating smoke, gunfire, booming cannons, and chaos. Men in blue and men in gray fought one another without mercy. A man's head was blown off right beside me, and my clothes were stained with blood. I came out of my trance to hear my nearly hysterical history teacher trying to wake me. Shaking with shock, I told her what I'd seen, and the interpreter accompanying our group had stared at me in amazement as I accurately described the battle as it took place where we were standing. Some of the kids thought it was a trick, that I was trying to get attention and had planned the whole thing. The interpreter knew better and so did my teacher. They saw the drops of blood staining my shirt and trousers, and both of them were close enough to me to smell the acrid, smoky aroma coming from my hair.

There were other incidents—many of them. I once saw Lincoln and his wife coming down the stairs in the White House. They were having some sort of disagreement, and I decided at once that I did not like Mrs. Lincoln. And I saw the doppelganger of our high school principal get up and walk away from his body while the real principal sat working at his desk. The next day he died of a heart attack.

I opened my eyes just in time to see my pretty Marie walk over to me. "Rick, I'm going down to the canoe landing," she said. "Do you want to come?"

I shook my head. "I'm still feeling pretty lousy," I told her. "I think Dad broke an arm."

She frowned a little. "Still no answer on the cell phone?"

"None," I replied. "You go ahead. I'll either be here or back in the car."

Marie kissed me lightly on the forehead and hurried away. I relaxed for a few minutes on the bench and then slowly climbed to my feet, cradling my sore arm. I headed for the entrance of the fort— and instead stepped out into a cloudy winter morning underneath breathtakingly huge fir trees still dripping from a recent fall of rain. I stopped in shock. Where was I?

The stillness around me was incredible. Modern life seemed very far away, especially when a group of men in buckskins came out of the fort, following a familiar face I'd often seen reproduced in history books. It was the face of Captain Clark. And in the group was another famous face—that of Sacagawea, with a little boy on her back.

"Don't just stand there lollygagging! Or don't you want to see the whale?" one of the men called to me. I followed them obediently, amazed by this latest time slip. The group accepted me unquestioningly, and I wondered in a bemused fashion which member of the Corps they believed me to be as I jogged along the path. I helped load up log canoes and soon found myself in one with Sacagawea, her husband, and the Captain. Wow, I thought, grabbing a paddle as we set off from the landing site.

Captain Clark was aiming to take us to Clatsop to hire a guide, but we hit a heavy wind from the northwest when we arrived in the bay. Such were the high waves produced by the wind that we were obliged to pull the canoes into a small creek instead. We traveled up the creek until we could go no further and then left our canoes and proceeded afoot. Clark led us past a pond to a large creek that still had a small log canoe he'd stashed away on a previous trip.

We crossed the creek three at a time in the canoe and climbed up a ridge. I gaped then at the sight of a large herd of elk, the likes of which had not inhabited Oregon in more than a hundred years. Always availing himself of the opportunity to hunt, Clark split us up, and we managed to bring down an elk, though two injured ones got away. By then it was dusk—too late to chase injured elk—so Clark had the single elk dressed, and we carried it with us as we headed down the creek to the shore. There, we made a driftwood fire, ate roasted elk, and camped for the night. The evening was clear, and the moon shone brightly overhead. From the conversation around me, I gathered that it was the first clear night they'd had in two months. I took some teasing for my silence on this trip, and several times the men referred to me as "Potts." I dared not speak much for fear of disrupting the time slip or alerting the mind I was overshadowing to my presence.

The next day was rough. We woke to a frosty morning and hiked upstream to a crossing. From there, we headed down to a sandy beach where the walking was easier. We walked for three miles until we encountered a wide river flowing into the sea. Clark rounded up a Clatsop man in a wretchedly poor, dirty house and paid him two fishing hooks to take our party across the river.

On the far side of the river, Clark paused and stared for a long time at a dead skate that had floated in on the tide. Apparently, he'd never seen one before. All of us gathered 'round to observe the singular creature. Little Jean-Baptist gurgled and pointed at it from the pack on his mother's back. Then we continued another two miles, where we met up with the men Lewis and Clark had sent out to make salt. They had a well-made campsite for their work and were situated near four houses of the Clatsop and Tillamook people.

Clark hired a young Indian lad to guide us to the whale, and we proceeded around a huge promontory that projected nearly four miles out into the ocean. The beach—for want of a better word—was full of round, slippery stones. The hill loomed high above us as we walked, and we'd gone another two-and-a-half miles on those wretched stones when the guide halted suddenly and told us we could proceed no farther. We had to go up and around. I looked up, along with the rest of the party. Up and up my eyes went, and still I couldn't see the top of the mountain, hidden as it was by low clouds. The ascent appeared almost perpendicular in places, but the path pointed out by our guide seemed to follow an easy switchback pattern, so we agreed to leave the shore. A mistake, I decided about an hour later. The path become much worse as we ascended, and at one point I was forced to draw myself up by bushes and roots for nearly a hundred feet. It took us two exhausting hours to reach the top, but the view was worth it. We had to have climbed nearly twelve hundred feet up the perpendicular mountain, and the ocean slamming into the shore was now far, far below us. I gazed down at the breakers, feeling almost dizzy.

The indefatigable Clark was chatting to our local guide about some white earth he spotted below us, trying to analyze its properties and meandering on at length about French porcelain. I was too busy trying to catch my breath to listen to much of the conversation. About this time, a party of Indian men and women came up to us, loaded down with oil and blubber from the dead whale. A hopeful sign, I decided, as we left the top of the precipice and proceeded down another bad road. Fatigued by our journey and that terrible climb, we decided to camp for the night on a small run to the left of the road. The whale could wait until morning.

We were up early, and I was hungry as all get-out. We didn't have nearly enough food to satisfy everyone in the party, but we had at least enough to sustain us for the next part of the trip. We proceeded to the top of the next mountain and found an open place overlooking the sea. It was breathtakingly lovely. In front of us was a boundless ocean. To the north, the seas raged and pounded endlessly against the cliffs, and below our feet was the whole sweep of mountains, valleys, and meadows. I thought I saw the mighty Columbia River pouring itself endlessly into the ocean far to the north. To the south, we could see many sea stacks and prominent rocks, some covered with birds. Sacagawea came up beside me, and together we looked down and down toward the sea. "It is beautiful here," she said softly, and I nodded. Her little boy gave me a big drooling grin, showing what few teeth he had, and I grinned back and chucked him on the chin.

Our guide pointed to a village at the mouth of a river, which he said was near the place where the whale had beached itself. He also pointed out several other principal villages of the Tillamook people. Then Clark took us down a steep descent to a single house he had spotted, the only remains of an old Tillamook town. The house was in a notch immediately on the shore and was surrounded by a large number of irregular rocks. The waves roared and splashed and shattered among them spectacularly. Near this old town, Clark took us to look at several large canoes lying on the ground. I realized, to my shock and surprise, that the canoes were death ships. Each one held an oblong coffin along with a paddle and sundry articles that I assumed were the property of the deceased.

Then we moved on along the rocky, slippery path beside the sea. On one side of us were the rugged hills; on the other side, a sheer drop to the sea. There had apparently been many landslides in this vicinity caused by the heavy winter rains, and it was not hard to imagine another crashing down on our heads. One false step would send me plummeting into the ocean— not a nice proposition at this height and with those sharp rocks underneath. I shivered and walked very carefully indeed.

We passed over three such dismal places, fortunately without mishap, and arrived on a beautiful, sandy shore. There, the walking was easier. We strode along on the damp sand at the edge of the water, and it was not long before I saw two

TIME SLIP

behemoths rising above me. One I recognized as Haystack Rock at what would—in the present day—be Cannon Beach. The other was the skeleton of a massive whale, which had already been pillaged of every valuable part by the Tillamook Indians. Many tall, white bones stuck up from the sand, and I could see the basic shape of the monstrous creature of the sea. The history books speculated that it was probably the body of a blue whale that washed ashore in this place. Whichever it was, it was an awesome sight, even without its flesh. Everyone gasped and hurried over to look at the massive skeleton. Clark measured it and proclaimed that it was 105 feet long.

I walked up to the huge bones, already starting to bleach white in the stinging, salty sea air. I put my hand against a cold bone and glanced across the skeleton at Sacagawea, who was staring up and down its length with glowing, dark eyes.

And then my head started to swim, and my arm started to ache, and I fell backward and backward away from the scene, which swirled around in many colors and solidified at last into the anxious face of my wife. "Rick! Are you all right?" Marie asked, shaking my sore arm with an anxious look on her face. "You were just standing there in a trance of some kind. What is it? What happened? Is it your Dad?"

I shook my head, trying to bring myself back to the present. It wasn't easy. I could still hear Captain Clark's voice in the distance, asking the group to return to the village, where the Tillamook people were boiling whale blubber to extract oil.

"Don't get lost on me again!" Marie exclaimed, shaking my sore arm once more. Pain throbbed through me, bringing me completely back to myself. My eyes popped open as I realized what I had seen and what I had experienced.

"Oh, wow! You'll never guess what I saw!" I exclaimed.

At that moment, the cell phone rang. Marie pulled it from her purse and answered it. It was my Mom. My bride handed me the phone, and Mom told me that my father had fallen from the roof while cleaning the gutters and had broken his right arm and dislocated his shoulder. As she spoke, the pain in my right arm throbbed once and then disappeared.

"Dad's going to be just fine, honey," Mom said over the phone. "He's already home and resting comfortably. So don't interrupt your trip. I just thought you should know."

"Thanks, Mom," I said. We talked a little longer, and then I hung up the phone. So my presentiment had been right. As usual.

I relayed the news to Marie, and then we walked back toward the little museum store, away from the replica of Fort Clatsop.

Marie glanced sideways at me and said: "Want to tell me about it?" I knew she was referring to my latest time slip. I gave her an enormous grin and said: "Boy, do I ever!" And so I did.

26

Destiny

CRATER LAKE

It's not easy growing up with destiny—either as a name, or as a part of your fate. Especially when you feel you're actually pretty ordinary inside. But I had both, and at times, it made things quite uncomfortable.

When my mother died shortly after my birth, my father—a great chief of my people—swore never to take another bride. In that hour, he named me as his heir and the ruler of our tribe. Such a thing had never been done before—a female chief was unheard of. But somehow, my father, a stern man and one used to being obeyed, managed it. And in doing so—had he but known it—he dictated a lonely existence for his only child. The other children in the village were in awe of the one who would be their next chief, and never behaved naturally around me or were comfortable when I asked to join their games. I was set apart and turned to the wild creatures around me and the spirits of the earth and air for my companions. For I was one of the few who could see these creatures—nearly transparent and full of that special life-force that makes crops ripen and babies grow.

When I was not called upon to learn the arts of the very wise, or the more mundane tasks of hearth and home, I wandered the mountains and valleys of my home, which surrounded Giiwas, the Crater Lake. I learned everything I could from the spirits. They accompanied me everywhere, transparent shimmers of rain or sunshine, shining green spirits of trees and grasses, and mischievous spirits of the wind, blowing this way and that, whispering secrets into my ears. I learned where the bear kept her cubs, which trees were pure and which had black hearts, which herbs would heal and which would kill. I studied the ways of the fox and the heron and the sea otter, and much else besides.

And so even as a young woman, among my people I became known as a wise woman, and many came to me for advice and healing. Yet still, I was alone among many. For not one of my friends bore a human shape, and my father was a stern and distant figure.

One fine summer day I went for a walk through an alpine meadow in the mountains of the sky lord that stood adjacent to the lands of my father, which were ruled by the lord of the underworld. I was at the very top of the sky lord's mountain, the spirits of the wind whirling about me and small earth spirits popping out of the flowers to greet me. My hand was on the head of the wolf Trueheart, my constant companion, when I heard the sound of fierce snarling and the joyful, deep-toned laughter of a warrior. I was startled, for I knew of none who came to this high place save myself. The sounds came from the far side of a copse of trees, and I would have been frightened save for the calm, happy demeanor of Trueheart and the cheerful flittings of the transparent beings who rode the wind. Following the lead of my companions, I drew a calming breath and slowly made my way to the meadow. There I stood, half-hidden behind a great bramble bush, and looked out upon the source of the commotion.

Three bear cubs were wrestling with a tall, ruggedly handsome man. His dark hair was caught back by a leather thong and hung in a long tail down his back. His chest and arms were bare and filled with lean, hard muscle. He wore buckskin pants of pure white doeskin decorated with gold and jewels the like of which I had never seen. They glowed with the light and fire of the sky— yellow and light blue and a translucent white that sparkled with all the colors of the rainbow. And he wore a chain around his neck on which hung another of the rainbow-colored jewels. One of the bear cubs was pawing it, and the man laughed again, a deep chuckle that made me smile. He swung the cub up and around while its brothers growled in mock fierceness and leapt on the man's moccasins.

The bushes swished beside me, and the mother of the cubs stepped into the gap and thrust her head under my hand in greeting. We were old friends, Mother Bear and I, and I knew her family well. Yet never before had I seen this man who played so freely with her children. The sight of him made my heart hammer and my knees weaken. I had not known that such a man could exist, and yet there he stood—or rather rolled—in the field in front of me.

Mother Bear gave a soft growl and immediately the man was on his feet and the cubs lined up neatly to one side of him, as if their mock battle had not taken place at all. The warrior bowed gracefully to Mother Bear, but his eyes were upon me, shining with the same intense curiosity as my own. His eyes were hazel-brown with green and yellow speckles. Amazing eyes. I found myself flushing red under his regard, quite unable to speak.

"Here, Mother Bear, are your little ones, as safe now as when you left them in my care," the warrior said.

"I thank you, Lord Skell," Mother Bear replied in her own tongue, full of grunts and growls.

Lord Skell. My heart leapt in awe and fear, for he was the god of the air, one to be esteemed and worshiped from afar. Yet he was here now, in as mortal a form as I.

"And wh . . . who is your fair companion?" Lord Skell asked, and I was startled by the small stammer I heard in his voice, so strange in such an awe-inspiring figure. I was further astonished to see a flush on his own face, so like the one on mine. Astonishment overcame shyness, and I whispered: "My name is Destiny."

"Destiny," he repeated softly. "The daughter of the great chief who lives on the slopes of Giiwas?"

"Y . . . yes," I stammered, flushing more deeply.

"I have heard much of you from my friends," Lord Skell said, reaching up to catch and entwine a few of the wind spirits around his long-fingered hands. "Fair one, keeper of destiny, I greet you," the lord of the sky said formally, and he bowed to me. To me. A simple, ordinary human girl.

Our eyes locked for a timeless moment that seemed to my fast-beating heart to last for centuries. Then Mother Bear broke the spell between us, trotting out to inspect her cubs, and Trueheart followed behind to jealously inspect the warrior who had captured my attention. Skell laughed and greeted the wolf in his own tongue. Then he came to me and took my hand, drawing me out of the shadows under the trees and into the fair light of the happiest afternoon I had ever lived. We walked through the flowery meadow and talked of many things, and it was only when dusk came that Skell reluctantly returned to his duties, gazing for another long moment into my eyes before he leapt into the air and vanished in a smattering of small flashes of rainbow light.

I danced home in deep delight, my head in the clouds with Skell, my heart already sore at the pain of parting with this one who had claimed my heart in a single glance. Yet all the time I knew that I was just an ordinary girl, though perhaps a wise one, and would probably never see him again.

It rained the next day, and I did not leave my village or wander the hills. Instead, I sat in council with my father, judging the daily matters of our people, and then spent the evening visiting the sick with our medicine man, using the herb lore learned from the earth spirits to ease pain and promote healing.

The next day brought a mighty visitor to our humble village. A dark man with a twisted face and bold, wicked eyes. He accosted me on my way to the stream to fetch water for the daily chores, knocking the pitcher from my hands and taking me by the shoulders in a bruising grip.

"Let me go," I said fiercely, trying to break away.

"I will never let you go, Fair One," he said. Hearing Skell's endearment on this evil man's tongue made my skin crawl. "For I am Llaos, king of the underworld, and you are Destiny, daughter of the great chief. I have seen you from my throne on top of the mighty Giiwas, and I have chosen you to be my queen."

I struggled fiercely against his strong grip. "I will not be your queen. Not now, not ever!" I ducked suddenly, pushing against the iron muscles of his stomach with both hands, and managed to break free. I ran back to the village on shaking legs, accompanied by the evil sound of Llaos's laughter.

"You will be mine, Destiny," he called after me. "It *is* your destiny!"

I fell to my knees in the dense bushes beside the house I shared with my father and retched. Around me, the shining green spirits of the trees and bushes swirled indignantly around me. Tiny, invisible hands stroked my hair and cheeks comfortingly, and Trueheart appeared suddenly from the trees, summoned by the breeze. He went at once to fetch my father, who helped me to my feet and listened sternly to my story.

"Llaos is a strong spirit, daughter. It is not wise to cross such a fierce one when we live in the shadow of his mountain. But if you do not care for him, I will not consent to the match," my father said.

My whole body shook at the very thought of it. "I will not have him," I gasped, and all the spirits of the earth and air gathered around me, buzzing and hissing and howling their agreement. Their reaction was so strong that even my father, usually deaf and blind to their presence, seemed to sense that they had sided with me.

"It is just as well," my father said. "For you could not rule the underworld and be chief of our people. And to be chief is your destiny."

What if I wish for a different destiny, I thought silently as my father helped me into our house. *One of my own choosing?* But I said nothing aloud.

Father kissed my forehead, poured me a cup of water, and then returned to his duties, while Trueheart lay guarding the doorstep. I thought of Skell, of the alpine valley where we had met, of the spirits of wind and rain and air that were my friends. Oh, how I wished for a different destiny. How I wished it had been Skell who had met me on the river path and asked for my hand in marriage. How different would my response have been.

King Llaos returned to the village that evening, his dark, twisted form framed by red fire. He was accompanied by many of the foul, writhing denizens of the deep lake that was the seat of his kingdom and his home. He came to my father and to the tribal council and demanded the hand of Destiny—my hand— in marriage, to live with him at the bottom of Giiwas as queen of the underworld.

My father said no. The council said no. I said no.

Llaos threw back his head and cursed every one of us by name, his whole body shaking with his fury. Above him, the sky darkened, and swirling clouds of ash blotted out the moon and stars. Around him, the fire framing the king and his companions grew brighter until it blinded the eyes and the red flames grew so hot they sizzled the skin. And then the ground started to shake.

I stumbled over to my stern father and gripped his arm, pleading silently with him to forgive me for my part in this trial. He covered my hand with his and stood tall and proud as above us, the mountains around Giiwas came awake, one by one.

"Oh, Skell, lord of the air," I sobbed softly, fearing I would never see him again after this evil night.

My father heard my prayer, though he did not, at the time, discern its true meaning. He threw back his proud head and cried loudly: "Skell, lord of the air, help us in our time of need!"

And Skell heard him. He heard both of us. A flash of lightning struck the ground beside the council fire, and riding it came my magnificent, handsome Skell. He stood before the lord of the underworld, his own form blazing with white light as different from the foul red light of Llaos as sunlight is from fire.

"You shall never have Destiny for your queen," Skell cried in a massive voice, loud as a thunderstorm. "She belongs to the air and the light."

"You mean she belongs to you," Llaos said sarcastically, and the earth shook so fiercely that all the humans around the council fire fell to their knees.

"That too," Skell said calmly, holding up his hand. A lightning bolt appeared in it, sizzling with white fire.

Llaos raised his own arms, and a spear of molten lava appeared in his grip. Then the lords of the air and the underworld flew up and up above the trees to stand on their respective mountains and do battle over me—Destiny. Just an ordinary human girl.

The whole village fled before the fierceness of the battle, as fire and lightning flew between the two gods, and one after another the mountains blew their tops, ash pouring into the sky and lava pouring down. While my people ran one way, I ran another, accompanied by Trueheart and all the spirits of the earth and air who were my friends. My one thought was to get to Skell, to aid him in any manner I could. Above me, the gods hurled huge rocks at one another, and bolt after bolt of dazzling white and sinister red flew from their hands. The ground shook constantly under my feet as I ran toward the mountain where I had first met Skell, and it was only Trueheart's sure-footed presence that saved me from being swept away by a massive landslide.

Dawn came finally, but the light of the sun was obscured by the terrible black cloud of ash that rose from the mountains. And still Llaos and Skell did battle. Daylight made my going easier, but I now found myself hiding as company after dark company

DESTINY

of foul beings arose from the Crater Lake and swarmed up the sky lord's mountain on either side of me. When I reached a ridge overlooking my tribal lands, I saw white spirits of the air swarming up Giiwas in pursuit of Llaos, and I urged them on with my whole heart.

I was trembling with exhaustion and fear, covered by dirt and ash and sweat when I stumbled into the alpine valley where first I saw the god of the air. And there my eyes met a terrible sight. The worst of Llaos's demons, his second in command, was creeping up the side of the massive rock on which Skell stood, aiming yet another bolt of white lightning at Llaos. The creature's many tentacles made short work of the climb. In one of them it held a stone knife.

"Skell!" I screamed. "Look out!"

The god of the air whirled when he heard my voice, but the warning came an instant too late. For the dark lord's denizen struck him in the chest, even as I screamed, and ripped out his heart.

Skell gave a choking cry, and his body tumbled from the mountain peak and fell into the tall grass and flowers of the meadow, almost at my feet. Laughing in triumph, the demon swarmed down the peak and headed for Llaos Rock, carrying Skell's still-beating heart.

"No!" I screamed, flinging myself beside my fallen lord. "No!"

He lay so still and pale, with a gaping, bloody hole in his chest, yet he was still handsome in death. Or was it death? Could a god really die? Mayhap, if his heart were restored, he would yet live?

I kissed his pale lips over and over in a frenzy, then took up his cold hand and swore to do what I could. "Just hold on, my darling. Hold on."

I left swarms of earth and air spirits to guard Skell's body and ran to the edge of the ridge. Around me, lava still spewed from the mountain peaks, and the earth trembled as the lord of the underworld gloated in triumph.

I raised both my arms and called to the spirits of the wind, my friends: "I am only an ordinary girl, but today I must be more. If you would have your lord live, than carry me as you do him. Carry me to the place where they have taken his heart!"

I didn't think it would work. But despair made me desperate.

To my surprise, the winds answered me, blowing round and round, harder and harder until I was lifted off my feet, high into the ash-smothered air. I coughed again and again, then covered my mouth and nose with a piece of buckskin torn from my clothing. The heat around me was oppressive, but I didn't care. The spirits of the wind swirled around me, carrying me over mountain peaks and lava flows, over the deep blue waters of Giiwas itself, which appeared black and menacing in the wrath of its lord. And there, chortling and dancing atop Llaos Rock, waving a still-beating heart in one tentacle, was the dark lord's second in command.

"Down there," I called to the spirits of the wind, and they obeyed. I swooped in like an eagle and tore the heart from the beast before he saw me coming. Then I was up and away, flying back toward my lord, while the beast howled and raced after me with supernatural speed. King Llaos screamed too from his throne on the edge of the crater and urged his minions after me. But the spirits of the sky were faster, and suddenly I was falling gently into the alpine meadow and stumbling over to my lord, his heart still beating softly against my hands.

I knelt beside Skell and pushed his heart back into the gaping hole in his chest. For a moment, I thought it was no good. That Skell truly was dead, in spite of the beat I had felt in his heart. Then the wound closed beneath my hands, and Skell coughed once, twice, and sat up. He stared blankly into my eyes for a moment and then gazed past me. His eyes widened at once, and he threw up a hand, grabbed something invisible in the air beside my head, and yanked downward. Behind me, the trees at the edge of the meadow fell down upon the tentacled monster, crushing it utterly. Then Skell threw both his arms around me and flew us both up to the top of the peak, where he had stood before. Keeping one arm tightly around my waist, he blazed with more than fire. He was as fierce and hot as the sun itself, and Llaos screamed and screamed again as bolts of sunfire rained down upon him. The spirits of the air swarmed up and over the rim of the crater, blazing as brightly as their lord, and fought mightily with the denizens of the underworld.

Then Skell leapt again into the air, leaving me to watch alone on the mountain peak as he called up a mighty sword that blazed with the fires of the sun. He rose up and up over Giiwas, finally bringing the sword down on the neck of the king of the underworld, sweeping his head from his shoulders in one mighty blow. The denizens of the deep screamed in terror when their dark lord fell and then plunged desperately into the deep blue waters of the lake, retreating to their kingdom far below. And Skell cut the body of the dark lord into pieces and fed it to the creatures of the deep. Then he threw down the head of Llaos, which landed in the depths with a mighty spout and bubbled up and up again in one last blaze of molten fire to harden at last into a large, black rock that rose several hundred feet from the dark waters of the lake.

As Skell's army laughed and danced and sang in victory, the lord of the air flew back to the mountain peak and swept me up into his arms. In spite of my bedraggled appearance—or perhaps because of it—he kissed me again and again, swirling both of us up through the dark cloud of ash into the fair light of the sun, and dancing with me on top of a rainbow in sheer, unadulterated joy.

There is not much more to tell. I would not be parted from my lord Skell, nor he from me, not after all we had been through together. My decision enraged my stern father, for it meant that I would be the queen of the air rather than chief of our people, as he had vowed. It was not until the spirit of my mother appeared to him in a dream and told him that this indeed was my true destiny that Father was reconciled to the match. He named my cousin as his successor in my place. And so I married Skell and went to live in the air as his queen, and all the spirits of the earth, the water, and the sky rejoiced in our happiness. I had found my true destiny, and it was everything I could ever wish for. And all that I would ever need.

27

The New Neighbor

I told Millie right from the start that our new neighbor was a bad one. Mr. Elgin lived in an apartment over his new dry goods store, and he seemed to prefer the nighttime. We never saw him out in the street before dusk. He was a tall, darkly handsome man with a face as white as new milk and a bit of an accent I couldn't place. He was very thin but very strong, almost supernaturally so.

I watched him on the evening he moved into the apartment next door to our boardinghouse. He got very angry with the movers when they jostled the six-foot-long box he had most carefully placed in the center of the wagon. I hated that box on sight. It looked just like a coffin to me, and my eyes burned red for several minutes after seeing it for the first time.

Mr. Elgin hired a local boy to take care of his store during the day. Billy was a good lad who'd grown up on a ranch outside town, but he wasn't bright enough to question his employer's odd habits. Billy took a room in our boardinghouse, and Millie took a motherly interest in him and made sure he was well fed.

I soon noticed that Mr. Elgin had a rather hypnotic effect on people. Whenever he appeared in the store after dusk, folks bought twice as many items as they intended. And many of the women ended up inviting him to dinner at the local restaurant, which was very strange, considering many of them were happily married.

Millie tutted over the situation, but what could you do? It was a free country, and if the local ladies wanted to make fools of themselves over a tall, dark stranger, that was their business—and their husbands'.

Mr. Elgin tried his hypnotism on me one late afternoon when I went next door to buy some nails to fix up the new-fangled water closet my wife insisted on having in the house for our boarders, but I was immune to those dark eyes with the red glint in their center. He looked rather chagrined that he couldn't persuade me to buy a very expensive and completely unnecessary plow for the farm-garden Millie kept in back of the boardinghouse. "What do we need a plow for? A spade and shovel work just fine," I told Mr. Elgin crisply as I paid a few pennies for the nails. That was the last time I patronized his store, and I forbade Millie to step foot inside it. Better to jog across town to the other dry goods store than to put oneself voluntarily in the presence of Mr. Elgin.

Millie laughed at me, but she could tell I was truly worried about the man, so she promised to keep away. She had enough to do cooking and cleaning up after the boarders. So that was all right.

It wasn't long after Mr. Elgin appeared that an illness spread through town. It mostly affected the womenfolk. They'd go all white and glassy-eyed, and red marks would appear on their throats or sometimes their wrists. The local doctors were baffled and tried every remedy they knew, to no avail. The disease continued to spread.

You could tell folks had the disease by the languid way they walked about town, and their too-pale faces. A couple of the ladies died after the local doctor tried bleeding the disease out of their bodies. So they stopped that technique and tried using elixirs to strengthen the blood. This seemed to offer the stricken some relief, but the epidemic continued to grow, in spite of the new treatment, and two more people died, their bodies white and stiff as if drained of all blood.

I quickly noticed that Mr. Elgin grew almost ruddy in appearance whenever someone in town fell ill. I also noticed that it was most often the women who invited him to dinner that suffered from the mysterious disease. I grew suspicious then and decided to check up on things myself.

Kissing Millie goodbye, I harnessed our two big workhorses and drove all the way out to the family ranch to visit my little Scottish grandmother. When I was a wee fellow, she'd told me stories about evil creatures that only came out at night and drank the blood of humans, and I was beginning to wonder if Mr. Elgin might be one of them.

Granny was thrilled to see me, but not so thrilled when she heard about Mr. Elgin. Her face grew positively grim when I told her about the illness sweeping through the town and the symptoms exhibited by the afflicted. Together, we consulted an old tome she'd brought west with her when she and granddad traveled the Oregon Trail. Granny turned to the section entitled "On Dark and Foul Creatures" and read me the passage aloud. In summary, it said that there were evil creatures called *vampyren* or *revenants* that returned from the grave to prey upon the living. They slept during the day in coffins filled with the dirt from their grave and walked abroad at night. To stave off a return to death, they drank the blood of living humans. You could protect yourself against the beings using garlic and holy objects, according to the book, but you could kill them only by plunging a wooden stake through their heart and removing their head.

"Sounds like your Mr. Elgin," Granny said, closing the book. I nodded grimly. So it did. I felt a sudden sense of urgency to return home. Millie was surrounded by all the boarders living in our house, but I still didn't like the thought of her living and working next door to Mr. Elgin. Our source said that vampires often killed their victims. The thought terrified me.

It was late, and I was forced to spend the night with my grandparents. But I woke at dawn, harnessed the horses, and headed for Baker City as fast as I could. It was dusk when I turned down the little alley behind the boardinghouse and pulled to a stop outside the barn. As I jumped off the seat of the wagon, Billy came running up to me.

"Oh, Mr. Porter, your wife is sick," he exclaimed. "She took sick last night after you left, and the doctor thinks she's got the plague, same as the other folks in town."

Alarmed, I threw the reins to Billy and asked him to put away the horses and the wagon. Then I ran into the boardinghouse, heading for the rooms reserved for Millie and me. Millie lay sleeping in bed, and from the doorway I could see the red marks on her throat where Mr. Elgin had sucked her blood. I was filled with a blinding fury, and it took several moments to calm down enough to wake my wife and find out what had happened. I could tell at once that Millie had been hypnotized by the creature calling itself Mr. Elgin. She spoke in fits and starts, saying she was out picking tomatoes for dinner the previous

THE NEW NEIGHBOR

evening and could remember nothing after greeting Mr. Elgin, who was taking the night air in the backyard of the dry goods store. Frankly, I was surprised she remembered that much.

Tenderly, I laid Millie back down to sleep. I tucked a great many cloves of garlic in the bed with her and placed Granny's cross around her neck. Then I went out back to the woodpile and started splitting logs and filing the pieces down into very, very sharp stakes. I was going vampire hunting. If Granny's book was correct, the vampire might very well visit Millie again tonight. And I would be ready for him.

It was almost midnight when I heard the first hypnotic sounds coming from the backyard. It sounded like someone humming a high-pitched tune, and it had a startling affect on Millie. Her eyes popped open, and she sat bolt upright. Her gaze was misty and unseeing, yet she hopped out of bed with ease and floated gracefully across the floor. I followed her, wooden stake in one hand and mallet in the other. Millie swept quickly through the large kitchen and out the back door. The strange, almost-singing sound increased in intensity as I hurried after her, and then stopped as Millie stepped into the vegetable garden. A dark figure in a sweeping black cloak was waiting for her. Its back was to me as it swept Millie into its arms. It bent its head, sharp canines gleaming in the moonlight, and then recoiled when it saw Granny's silver cross around my wife's neck.

I took two silent steps forward and thrust the stake into the creature's heart with all my strength. It started bolt upright in pain, dropping Millie to the ground. I smashed the mallet against the stake, forcing it deeper into the vampire. Mr. Elgin gave a single, high-pitched whine like that of a wolf in pain and then collapsed onto the ground. I grabbed my axe and lopped off his head right then and there. There was no blood on the axe when I returned it to the woodpile. I suppose Mr. Elgin had no blood of his own, I reasoned. Only that of his victims. I carried Millie into the house and tucked her back into bed. Then I wrapped Mr. Elgin's head and body in a couple of thick blankets, put them in the wagon, and drove the dead vampire out of town to a distant canyon. There, I set the body afire and watched it burn through much of the night. And that was the end of Mr. Elgin.

The local doctors were amazed at the way the plague suddenly vanished from Baker City. All the victims soon were better, and no one ever associated disease with the appearance or disappearance of the mysterious Mr. Elgin. Folks just assumed he'd gotten tired of life in the Wild West and headed back East. The only ones who ever knew the truth of the matter were Millie and my old Granny. And they never told a soul.

28

Close Encounter

WILLAMETTE FOREST

Highway 242 over the MacKenzie Pass was still blocked with snow the day I made the drive from Eugene to Bend over the Cascade Mountains. If it hadn't been, what happened wouldn't have happened, if you follow me.

I was on my way to stay with friends in Bend. It was the first vacation I'd allowed myself to take in several years. It's hard to get away when you run your own business. But I'd allowed myself to be talked into the trip, and as I set out for the scenic drive along the MacKenzie River highway, I grew excited at the prospect of a whole week of relaxation and enjoyment. Starting right now!

That stretch of highway has got to be my favorite in the whole world. Traveling along the rapids-filled MacKenzie River, past gorgeous farms and covered bridges. Then up into the forested slopes of the Cascades, with the massive Sitka spruce and Coastal redwood and Douglas fir. I stopped here and there to snap a few pictures or take a breath of fresh air, and a couple of times I cursed myself for forgetting to pack my fishing pole. The fishermen were out in force on this lovely, late spring day.

I'd really been looking forward to the drive along Highway 242 and had planned a prolonged stop at the Dee Observatory at the top of MacKenzie Pass, but it was not to be. Snow still blocked the road. Disappointed, I followed the highway to the left, heading up and up through forests that struck me as almost primeval in appearance, climbing through the upper reaches of the Willamette Forest and up and over Santiam Pass to the Route 20 fork leading down to Bend.

I had plenty of time to spare and pulled off the highway when I saw a small sign for the Sahalie Falls. Sounded like a nice place to take a break. I parked my SUV in the lot and then headed along the path and down the steps toward the falls. I wasn't expecting the thunder and mist that struck me almost as soon as I stepped onto the walkway, skirting a drift of snow that lay across the path. I quickly caught a glimpse of a massive falls, absolutely pouring water at a tremendous rate down and down into a deep pool. The water was so clear it looked aqua! I gaped and snapped many pictures in sheer delight.

The trail led downward toward the Koosah Falls, and steps had been cut into the steep descent to make walking easier. Snowdrifts covered with pine needles were everywhere, and the tall pines were absolutely festooned with bright green moss. It was an amazing, primitive place. Far below me, the river boiled and rushed with amazing speed down the mountain, still that amazing light-blue color under the white rapids. I wouldn't want to fall in there, I thought, carefully negotiating a mound of snow and landing on the other side in mud created by the melt water. It covered my shoes completely. Yuck! And that's when I saw them. Two gigantic footprints, absolutely enormous in size, just in front of me. And still oozing mud, as if freshly made.

I'd heard of Bigfoot, of course. Who hadn't, growing up in Oregon? But I'd always thought of it as a mythical creature. Seeing two huge prints like that in the middle of a snow-strewn pathway deep in a forest at the top of the Cascades made something in my stomach twist. I kept staring at the footprints, as if staring would make them disappear. They had to be half again as large as my feet—and I'd always had big feet for a man.

I looked up finally and gazed ever so cautiously around me. To my right was the roaring river, and to my left huge snowdrifts covered fallen trees, burying massive trunks to a depth of six feet or more. Beyond the muddy hole in which I stood was another drift of snow, packed down by the feet of many hikers so that any individual tracks could not be distinguished.

For some reason, I kept thinking of deer and other wild creatures that—just by standing still—could remain hidden in plain view. With all these massive trees around me, a Bigfoot could be standing only a few feet away and I wouldn't see or hear it over the massive roar of the falls. The thought frightened me. You hear stories of Bigfoot going mad and killing people in its territory; though just as often you hear stories of its passivity.

I stood for a long moment, undecided whether to take my chances and continue hiking through the increasingly heavy snowdrifts to the lower falls, or to turn back. Some instinct was urging me to turn back. My flesh was crawling on both arms and legs, as if wild eyes were watching my every move. I wanted out of there! I turned and climbed back up and over the snowdrift.

Suddenly, my foot slipped and I fell, sliding down the drift and landing seat first in a pile of wet pine needles and mud on the other side. My first emotion was annoyance. I wouldn't be fit to be seen at my friend Mike's place at this rate. My second thought

CLOSE ENCOUNTER

was that the strange, hairy tree trunks in front of me looked a lot like legs. Massive legs. Legs that ended in huge, hairy, bare feet. Feet that gave off an odd animal smell of sour sweat and musk. I looked up and up, past a mammoth, hairy chest, into the strangely flattened features and black eyes of a Sasquatch.

It reached down with massive hands and, before I could utter a squeak, grabbed me by the forearms and pulled me to my feet. Then it grunted, leapt straight up over the snowdrift to my right, and was gone into the gloom of the forest, just like that.

I gulped once, twice, trying to get some moisture into my dry mouth and throat. Then I ran up the muddy stairs and across the boardwalk, straight out into the parking lot. My heart thundered against my ribs and I plopped my muddy rear end into the driver's seat, wheels squealing as I pulled out of the parking lot.

I shook like a leaf the whole way up and over the pass and down the far side of the mountains. I paused briefly in Sisters to change my dirty clothes, mop up the wet and muddy driver's seat, and eat a hamburger. Then I drove the rest of the way into Bend and pulled at last into my friend Mike's driveway.

For a long, long time, I just sat there as the engine cooled and Mike peered out the front window curiously. In my mind, I kept seeing the blunt, primitive face of the creature we call Sasquatch, and feeling its massive, strong hands pulling me to my feet. As the front door opened and Mike came out to greet me, I wondered briefly if I should tell him about my close encounter. Nah, I decided, stepping out of the car and waving my hand to Mike's wife, who stood beaming in the doorway. They'd never believe me.

The Wanderer

PORTLAND

They borrowed a friend's car and filled it with their meager belongings when they got home from their honeymoon at the seashore. They were moving to Portland to start their new life together. Sarah was a nurse, and Jimmy was a retired soldier turned store manager.

Sarah met Jimmy in the hospital after he was mustered home from the war overseas. He had a severe hip injury that wasn't healing properly. Sarah was newly assigned to Jimmy's ward, and they'd taken to each other at once. It was not quite love at first sight, but it was certainly friendship. And it wasn't long before a romance bloomed between them. They were enough alike to get along but not so much that it got boring. Both families were pleased with the match. Within a few months, Jimmy was leading Sarah down the aisle at the local church after the minister pronounced them husband and wife.

On the day they wed, Jimmy gave Sarah his Distinguished Service Cross award to keep as a symbol of his love and his vow to honor and cherish her. The Distinguished Service Cross was the second-highest military decoration that could be awarded to a member of the United States Army. Her father told Sarah that it was awarded for extraordinary heroism. Sarah wore the cross on a chain around her neck night and day as a symbol of courage and to remind herself how very lucky they were. Jimmy would probably always limp in bad weather, but he made it through his wartime duties relatively unscathed.

Jimmy had saved most of his soldier's salary, and it was enough to get them started with a new life in Portland. Jimmy would manage his cousin's grocery store, and Sarah would work in the local hospital. There was a modest apartment over the store that Jimmy's cousin rented to them for a song. Their car full of belongings would fit nicely into that small space. It was a good start to a new life, Sarah thought with a smile, listening to her handsome husband whistling in the driver's seat beside her.

They were entering the city when Sarah saw a ragged old man striding stiffly along the side of the road. He was one of several commuters walking into town, but to Sarah, he stood out with great clarity, as if he were outlined with a wicked red light. His ancient face was withered almost to the bone, his longish hair white and scanty. And his eyes! The terrible eyes. They were the eyes of a man who had looked into the bottomless pit of despair and saw no hope of redemption.

For a moment, Sarah's gaze locked with that of the old man, and her mind was overwhelmed with images. She saw a body lying on once-velvet grass, its head brutally bashed in and its rough, primitive garments stained with bright red blood. Black roiling clouds descended on the scene, crushing the surrounding trees beneath a howling wind. Trunk after trunk broke off and flew away as lightning scarred the sky. Beneath the body, flowers and grass withered wherever the red blood flowed, until the body lay in a circle of black decay. It seemed the whole world mourned this one particular death.

The despair and horror of the scene flickering through her mind stole Sarah's breath away. She tore her gaze from the old man with a gasp of fear, clutching the Distinguished Service Cross hanging around her neck for courage.

One image lingered as she looked away. It was the face of a man standing at the edge of the clearing with a blood-stained rock in his hands. His beautiful, terrible face was twisted with consternation—a ghastly mixture of jealous hatred and defiance. The man's face was as handsome as a god and as foul as a demon.

"Are you all right, hon?" Jimmy asked, glancing at Sarah in concern as he slowed the car to make a turn.

"Oh, yes. No," she stammered, taken aback by this brief encounter. "Just something I saw. An old man."

"Which one," Jimmy asked with a laugh, waving toward the side of the road. Sarah realized that half a dozen old men were trotting along the sidewalks, some with lunch pails and others with sacks on their shoulders. Not one of them was the man she'd just seen entering Portland.

"Never mind. It was nothing," Sarah said, forcing a laugh. "Are we nearly there?"

"About ten minutes," Jimmy said.

And ten minutes later, they were parked outside their new home, transferring their belongings to the upstairs apartment. Jimmy and his cousin carried in the heavy pieces while Sarah unpacked boxes and directed the arranging of the furniture. In the ensuing bustle of moving, the memory of the old man slipped completely from Sarah's mind.

The new apartment was cozy and warm. Sarah loved it immediately. Jimmy's cousin had painted the walls a light yellow color that worked perfectly with the curtains and quilt she'd stitched for their bedroom. Content with these and other small miracles, Sarah set to work making the apartment into a home while her excited husband inspected every inch of the grocery store below.

The nightmares started on Sarah's first night in their new home. She woke up in a cold sweat, heart pounding fiercely, with no memory of the dream that had frightened her. There was no movement at all in the new bedroom, and the only sound was her husband's soft breathing beside her. All was peaceful and still, yet she was terrified and trembling, as if some malevolent presence had come into the room seeking to destroy her.

Courage, Sarah thought, clutching the Distinguished Service Cross around her neck, trying to calm herself. Sensing her distress, Jimmy reached for Sarah in his sleep and cuddled her close, comforting her. But it took Sarah a long time to fall back to sleep.

In the days that followed, Sarah unpacked boxes and arranged things to her satisfaction. She was as happy as she'd ever been except for the baffling nightly nightmares. She had completely forgotten the incident with the old man.

They had been in their new apartment for a week when folks at the grocery store started talking about the Spanish flu. The disease was spreading through the poorer sections of town. People were sickening by the dozens, and the hospital wards were filling up. Sarah knew she was needed. She went at once to the local hospital, and they gladly welcomed a new nurse to help with the sudden epidemic. The elderly and the very young were the first to arrive and also the first to die. But even the sturdiest of individuals was susceptible to the virulent strain of flu that was sweeping through the city.

Sarah grew thinner each day. She barely had time to care for herself in the rush to tend to all the patients filling the hospital wards. Jimmy made all their meals at home and stood over his wife until she ate every bite. "You can't help others if you get sick," he told Sarah over and over.

Sarah fell into bed each evening, exhausted from rushing around all day, but still she woke in the middle of the night with a pounding heart from a nightmare she could not remember.

As the Spanish flu epidemic grew worse, the mayor banned all public meetings, including sporting events, church services, and school activities. The Civic Auditorium was adapted to care for the sick, as hospitals, funeral homes, and morgues were filled beyond capacity. Sarah was assigned to a ward in the auditorium, caring for those who might make a recovery. She fought for each life as hard as she could. It took a toll on her spirits whenever a patient succumbed to the illness, but she rallied herself and kept going. If even one survived, it was worth the effort.

In the ninth week of the epidemic, Sarah was switched to night duty. Jimmy insisted on escorting her to and from the auditorium, not wanting his wife walking alone through the streets at night. On the fourth night of the new schedule, they came face to face with an old man standing under a lamppost just outside the grocery store where Jimmy worked. His ancient face was withered; his long white hair was scanty. He was as thin as a skeleton, and he had bottomless eyes that knew only despair. Sarah gasped in recognition and gasped again when the man fainted at Jimmy's feet.

"Another Spanish flu victim," her soldier-husband said calmly, stooping to press a finger against the man's throat. "Thready pulse. He isn't in good shape. I'm not sure he'll make it through the night. We'd best bring him with us to the auditorium."

Jimmy stooped, lifted the frail figure, and tucked the man over his shoulder. He set off for the hospital, and Sarah followed a step behind, her heart pounding. She clutched the Distinguished Service Cross hanging from its chain. *Courage*, she thought as she remembered the vision she'd seen pouring from the old man when they entered Portland for the first time. Now she knew the cause of her nightmares. She had been reliving the vision each night in her dreams. The face of the emaciated old man had brought it all back.

Sarah didn't want to help him. She wanted to flee in the opposite direction as fast as she could. Who was this old man, and why did he seem outlined in red light even now, as he drooped over Jimmy's broad shoulder? Sarah knew her duty and would do it faithfully, but this old man frightened her. Evil seemed to pulse out of him. Was she the only person who could see it? Maybe she was going mad herself from stress and exhaustion.

The old man was assigned to Sarah's ward, and the doctor had him placed in a small alcove away from the other patients. The doctor said it was to give the ancient man privacy in his final hours, but he looked uneasy when he spoke, and Sarah wondered if there was another reason. Others equally ill had come and gone before this and had not been placed in seclusion. This old man inspired fear, even in an unconscious state. Sarah had yet to touch him, as the doctor had, but even from a distance he seemed rimmed with red light.

After taking the day nurse's report, Sarah walked through the ward, checking each patient. Then she steeled herself and stepped into the alcove with the old man. His breathing was ragged with the familiar rattle of death. His face was haggard and emaciated, though not as thin as she had first thought when she saw him swaying under the lamppost outside the grocery story. She reached for the old man's wrist to feel his pulse.

When Sarah touched him, the ward vanished. She could feel the unnatural chill of his skin and the ragged beat of his heart under her fingertips, but she was seeing an ancient battlefield. Men in chariots thundered across a plain, beating at enemy soldiers on the ground with swords and spears. Bodies were strewn everywhere. Blood stained the dirt and grass and small shrubs. A soldier fighting next to her was beheaded before her terrified gaze. A rearing horse kicked another soldier in the stomach and sent him flying. The clash of arms and screams in an unknown language filled her ears. Sarah could smell blood and death and sweat. Two men rolled on the ground in front of her, battering each other ruthlessly.

Sarah dropped the old man's wrist, gasping in fear. The ward reappeared before her eyes. She swayed and fell into a chair beside the bed, her own pulse pounding frantically in her throat and wrist. She clutched the Distinguished Service Cross as she stared at the ancient face on the pillow. Who was this man?

Sarah adjusted the blankets around her patient's body, careful not to touch him, and went back into the ward. She kept herself busy for almost an hour, caring for a few new arrivals. Then, reluctantly, she went back into the alcove to check on the old man.

As she stepped inside the shadowy space, she halted in astonishment. The man looked different. His hollowed cheeks were plumper then they'd been an hour ago, and he seemed to have fewer wrinkles. His white hair was thicker, too, and his arms weren't so thin. He looked younger. His breath was still uneven, and he was still obviously ill, but the death rattle was gone. What was going on?

Sarah stepped to the bedside, braced herself, and laid her fingers against the pulse at the old man's throat. The ward vanished as before, but the pulse under her fingers was stronger this time, and the vision before her eyes was different. She was in a crowded city full of stone houses and human waste. People as thin as skeletons were walking disinterestedly along the streets. Urchins were battling over a crust of bread they found on a refuse heap. A man staggered past Sarah carrying a dead rat, his eyes alight with anticipation. Here was food at last. One of the urchins saw the rat in the man's hands and shouted. Immediately, the whole gang charged the man, and he raced away with his prize, the children hot on his heels. An old woman picked up the dirty crust of bread left behind, chuckling with delight, and carried it through a nearby doorway. Sarah tore her gaze from the repulsive sight, her stomach turning. She looked out across barren fields, dusty and dead. There was nothing growing, no green anywhere. No water. It was a barren wasteland. The ferocious sunlight had burned everything away.

Sarah pulled her hand away from the old man and sat down in the chair. She was still frightened of him, of the red light that surrounded him. But she was also intrigued and puzzled. She'd seen a murder. She'd seen a war. And now she'd seen famine. These were terrible things—the curses of mankind. Why was

THE WANDERER

she seeing these visions, and what did they have to do with this old man? Thoughtfully, she tended to his needs and returned to the main ward.

Sarah dealt with a death, a seizure, and a high fever, one following right after the other. It was nearly two hours before she was free to check on the elderly man in the alcove. She wasn't sure what to expect when she stepped inside, but she certainly wasn't prepared for what she saw. The face on the pillow had filled out completely. The wrinkles were restricted to the forehead and eyes. The hair was gray now instead of white and much longer and thicker than before. The man's breathing was heavy but not ragged. He looked like a venerable grandfather, an individual just past his prime. He was aging in reverse! And to Sarah's gaze, he was still rimmed with red light.

The man moved his head on the pillow, restless. A fever still flushed his cheeks. Sarah brought him a cup of water and gingerly lifted his head so he could drink it. She felt the thick gray hair cushioning the strong skull, felt him lap the water. But all she could see were locusts. Millions and millions of locusts flew around her, eating everything in their path. The buzz of their wings was so loud she couldn't hear anything else. They bumped grotesquely into her hair, her body. They landed on her and crawled all over her skin. One tried to fly up her nose.

Doggedly, Sarah held on to the man's head until she felt the lapping cease. Carefully, she tipped the cup upright and laid the man's head back onto a softness that she assumed was the pillow. Then she pulled her hand away, and the locusts vanished.

Sarah put the cup down on the table so abruptly it splashed water onto the floor, but she didn't care. She was brushing herself all over; trying to wipe away the feeling of locusts crawling on her skin. She felt her cap, which was still miraculously in place. Were there bugs in her hair? No, everything felt normal. Sarah backed out of the alcove, physically revolted by the memory of the locusts.

Sarah avoided the alcove for a few hours, merely peeking inside at the man on the bed from time to time to make sure he didn't need any special care. Each time she looked, the man appeared younger, healthier, less likely to perish. But she knew she couldn't avoid him all night. She had a duty as his nurse.

Around 3:00 a.m., Sarah braced herself and walked back into the alcove to tend to her terminal patient. The man she saw now was middle aged. He had dark hair that was graying at the temples; a strong, proud face; and a cruel mouth. The wrinkles cut into his face now were those of anger, not mirth. His eyebrows were thick and almost joined across a prominent nose.

The man was still feverish, so she wetted a cloth and laid it across his broad forehead. Her fingers barely brushed his skin, but it was enough. The ward vanished, and she saw a medieval city with narrow streets. The smell of rot and vomit and something burning filled her nostrils. She saw a few bodies lying in a nearby alleyway covered in black boils, some of them still oozing blood and puss. Through the city gates, she glimpsed a flaming pyre. Stacks of dead bodies were being burnt by men with rags wrapped over their faces in an effort to ward off disease. A man lying next to the outer wall writhed with fever. She saw him vomit and scratch desperately at a black boil on his neck. Pus oozed over his hand. Sarah recognized the symptoms of the Black Death. She pulled her hand away from the man's forehead and stared into his face. As if he sensed her gaze, the man's eyelids fluttered but did not open. His head moved restlessly on the pillow, but he did not wake. Sarah stepped away and returned to her duties on the ward.

When Sarah returned near dawn, the face on the pillow was that of a very handsome young man in his early thirties. His skin was smooth, though angry wrinkles were already visible on his face. The man's mouth was proud and cruel, his chin sharp. Sweat dewed his forehead and cheeks. The fever had broken.

Sarah stepped forward and lifted the man's wrist. The pulse under her fingers was strong and sure as she gazed at an Egyptian temple filled with newly painted hieroglyphics. Inside the temple, an unusual confrontation was taking place. A dying priest writhed in agony from a snake bite while a lovely woman with the clothes and bearing of an ancient queen watched in grim satisfaction. The cruel set of her mouth reminded Sarah of the man on the bed. The face of the priest was so like that of the woman that Sarah knew he must be her brother. Another murder, Sarah thought. It was the second murder she'd seen in her visions.

Sarah released the man's wrist and found herself staring into a pair of black eyes. Now she recognized him. He was the man holding the rock whom she had seen in the first vision. A murderer. A man doomed to wander the earth for his terrible crime.

"You seem to have made a full recovery," Sarah said coldly, gazing defiantly into the handsome face. "We can release you right away. You can go home."

The young man considered her, his gaze cool and calculating. "I have no home," he said at last. "I am a Wanderer."

"Yes," Sarah said. "I have . . . seen . . . some of the places you have wandered. I think perhaps it is time for you to wander somewhere else."

The dark eyes narrowed for a moment. There was a red glint in their depths. Sarah's pulse thrummed with fear, but she held his gaze. Her hand strayed to the Distinguished Service Cross around her neck.

Suddenly, the young man relaxed and smiled. Sarah blinked, dropping her hand from the pendant in surprise. The man had a dazzling smile, rarely used. There was Eden in that smile.

"You have been kind and courageous," he said. "I will, as you request, wander somewhere else."

Sarah nodded and left the alcove. The day nurse had arrived. Sarah gave her report and, at the end, gestured toward the alcove. "And finally, it appears that Mr.—" She hesitated, wondering what she should call him. Before she could finish her sentence, the young man stepped out of the alcove. He was wearing a modern suit and carrying a hat. He looked like a prosperous farmer. His clothes had apparently aged in reverse with his body.

"Mr. Adamson," the young man said, nodding politely to the day nurse. Sarah's eyes widened appreciatively at this clever appellation.

"Mr. Adamson," she continued smoothly, "has made a full recovery and is ready to depart. I've left notes on the other cases on the desk."

"Thank you," said the day nurse, somewhat breathlessly, as she patted her hair and blushed, eyeing the handsome young man. "I'm *so glad* you've recovered, Mr. Adamson."

The young man nodded to the day nurse but did not reply. He followed Sarah through the impromptu wards of the auditorium and out to the street.

"Goodbye, Mr. Adamson," Sarah said. She did not offer her hand. "I trust we will not see each other again."

"No, we will not," the young man said. "But rest assured, I will not forget your kindness. And know that it is thanks to you that this epidemic will not grow worse. Goodbye, Sarah."

Sarah felt chills run down her arms when he said her name. No one had spoken her name in his hearing. But he knew it anyway.

There was nothing accidental about any of their meetings.

Sarah wondered if there was always one person chosen, whenever the Wanderer came to town, who could redeem the situation if they acted courageously, if they were willing to try. She did not ask the young man this question. She merely nodded and watched him turn away, heading toward the edge of town.

On impulse, she called out suddenly, "Mr. Adamson!"

The young man paused and turned around. He raised a questioning eyebrow.

"I hope that someday you will cease to wander," she said. "That you will find your way home."

"That I will find redemption?" he asked cynically.

Sarah reached up and unclasped the chain around her neck. She tossed the pendant to the young man. He caught it and stared at the Distinguished Service Cross in his hand. Sarah smiled, knowing that Jimmy would approve when she told him what she'd done.

"There is *always* a second chance at redemption," Sarah said. "We just need the courage to take it, Mr. Adamson."

The young man looked up suddenly, his mouth trembling. He nodded to her and then nodded to someone behind her. "Thank you," he said. He walked away.

Sarah turned and saw her courageous husband standing a few feet away. He'd come to escort her home. To make sure she was safe.

"That was the old man we rescued last night," Jimmy said quietly, taking her hand. It was not a question.

"Yes," said Sarah softly.

"I look forward to hearing his story," Jimmy said. Then he leaned over and kissed her forehead. "Well done, love."

30

Amhuluk the Monster

The warrior had heard the tales of Amhuluk the Monster all his life, but he discounted them. The elders claimed that a huge horned monster lived within a lake on the slopes of the Forked Mountain, far above the valley where the tribe dwelt. This seemed utterly improbable to the warrior's logical mind. Who had ever heard of such a creature, much less laid eyes on it? There were no eyewitnesses to his knowledge. How could the elders possibly know that such a monster existed?

The elders declared that any living creature stepping onto Amhuluk's land was drawn into his watery embrace and drowned on his enormous spotted horns. Even the trees along the shoreline, they said, had succumbed to the monster, their crowns lying upside down in Amhuluk's embrace. The monster's only friends were the dogs, which came and went at will in the shadow of the Forked Mountain.

The elders told the story of a father who lost two of his children to the monster when they wandered up to the lake to harvest roots and berries. Amhuluk had speared the children on his spotted horns and pulled them under the surface of the lake to drown. Their spirits had teased and taunted their poor father for six days, appearing with the mist and then vanishing beneath the mud whenever he pleaded with them to return home. The tribe avoided the Forked Mountain for fear of the monster.

The warrior chafed at such a restriction. It kept him away from the good hunting and gathering on the mountain slopes. The tales were told by old men who were too feeble to fight anymore. Why should he heed them? But everyone in his tribe kept away from the Forked Mountain, and so did he.

The warrior had been courting a lovely girl from a neighboring family, and she finally consented to be his bride. The couple soon welcomed three children into their home: two boys and a daughter in the middle. The warrior was proud of his young family. In his happiness, he forgot all about Amhuluk the Monster. The lake on the Forked Mountain seemed far removed from the good life he lived.

The warrior taught his young sons to hunt and showed all three of his children how to gather berries and roots and other edibles from the land. But there were two things the warrior failed to pass on to his children. The first was the tribe's restriction against the Forked Mountain. And the second was Amhuluk the Monster's love for dogs. These facts didn't matter to the warrior since they could not possibly have any impact on him or his family. So he never spoke of them to his children.

One day in late spring, the warrior's eldest son came home carrying a scruffy small dog that he had found wandering at the foot of the Forked Mountain. The creature had an adorable whiskered face and pleasing ways. His younger son followed the little beast around as if it were the master and not he, while his daughter adorned the dog with flower chains and passed it special treats from her plate when she thought no one was watching. As for his eldest son, he and the canine were inseparable. They wandered through the valley together, hunting and fishing and playing with the other boys.

As summer drew to a close, the dog grew restless and would vanish for hours each day, though it always returned by evening. The children were troubled by its frequent absences and spoke of tying it up so it could not wander. But no one else in the tribe restricted their dogs, and the warrior would not allow them to keep it contained. "He must be free to choose you, my sons, my daughter," the warrior told them. "If he does not, then he is no more than your slave."

One night, the dog failed to return. The children were devastated until it reappeared the next morning.

"We should follow him and see where he goes," the warrior heard his eldest son suggest to his siblings. "Then we will know, and we won't worry anymore."

A shadow passed over the warrior's heart when he heard his son's words, though he found no reason for his distress. The story of Amhuluk the Monster and his dog friends had slipped completely from his mind. What harm could come to the children by following a little scruffy dog? It might be a good thing, for it would ease the children's minds to know where their pet went each day. Yet somehow, the warrior could not shake the feeling that this course of action was not wise.

The next morning, when the dog trotted away, the children took their gathering baskets and followed, telling the warrior and his wife that they would return before dark. Their mother chuckled and said, "They are determined to solve this puzzle! I wonder what tales they will bring us tonight."

The warrior tried to smile in return, but a shard of ice had lodged itself in his heart. He wanted to run after his children and call them back. But this made no sense at all. He nodded curtly and then softened his face into a smile so his wife would not think he was angry. Casting one anxious look after the children, he gathered up his weapons and went out to hunt for game.

The warrior returned home mid-afternoon with a deer and found his wife cooking the evening meal. She kept glancing toward the forest with a worried frown. "The children haven't come home," she said as he unloaded his prize.

Before he could respond, they heard pounding footsteps and the thrashing of branches. Their eldest son burst forth from the forest path, his eyes wide with horror. The boy collapsed at his parents' feet, panting desperately.

"My son, what is it? What has happened?" the warrior cried.

"Something . . . something dreadful came near us," the boy gasped. "It has taken away my brother and my sister."

"Something dreadful? What was it? Where were you?" the warrior demanded, terror knotting his stomach. He stared desperately into his son's face, noting that the boy's skin was covered with blots, just like the spots on a monster's horns.

For the first time in years, the warrior remembered Amhuluk the Monster, who lived up on the mountain, and he also remembered the monster's fondness for dogs. The warrior knew what had happened even before his son replied.

"We were up on the Forked Mountain," his son said. "We followed the dog to the lake, where he met another dog that looked just like him. I think it was a littermate. While the dogs played, we began digging roots on the lakeshore. My sister noticed two strange spotted trees with pointed tops growing on the far side of the lake. We were curious. We'd never seen anything like them. We thought they might make good digging tools, so we walked around the lake to look at them."

The boy paused, his face working as he fought tears. "We were only halfway there when the spotted trees moved! A huge head lifted from the water, and we realized the spotted trees were horns. The creature rushed us, and we scrambled up the slope to get away. But it was too fast. It lifted my sister and my brother up on each of its horns and raced away across the lake."

The eldest son broke off, his face twisted in agony. Then he wailed, "I tried to follow, but I couldn't! So I ran here as fast as I could for help. Oh, Father!"

The warrior was already moving, fetching all of his weapons and flinging himself onto his horse. There was no time to waste. There was no telling what Amhuluk would do with two small children. If what the elders said was true, it might already be too late. But he would not say that in front of his wife and son.

The warrior rode as fast as he could toward the mountain, alternating between a canter and a walk so as not to founder his horse, which he had hand raised from a colt. Every time he slowed, his heart pounded with terror. Hurry. Hurry. Precious minutes were ticking away, and dusk came early in these mountains. It seemed to take forever to climb up to the lake along the rough deer track, for the tribe maintained no trails here.

The sun was setting over the mountain when the warrior saw the lake ahead of him. Tendrils of mist were already forming over the still surface of the water, which mirrored the towering peak above and the trees along its banks.

The warrior followed the footprints left by his laughing children only a few hours before. He turned right along the shoreline, scanning the ground for signs of his children and then lifting his eyes to search the waters for two sharp, spotted horns. He moved slowly and carefully, wondering how he would fight such a monster if it charged him. If its hide was too thick for arrows, he would need to use his knife or his axe.

The light was fading, and the fog was extending toward the shore when the warrior saw a muddy spot where the ground had been disrupted by the children's digging. He dismounted and moved toward the lakeshore with an arrow nocked on his bow, his knife close to hand.

Around him, nothing stirred. The lake was preternaturally still. There was no wind. He heard no whirr of wings or chirp of crickets. He'd stepped into a bubble of absolute silence. It made the warrior's skin crawl. The slightest breeze would have been as welcome as a song to his ears. The only sound was his breath, and even that seemed muted and far away. The air pressed on him like a thick blanket trying to smother him.

The warrior felt but could not hear his horse walking directly behind him. The animal was trembling, but it refused to leave its beloved master alone in this menacing place. If the monster confronted them, the horse would fight beside the warrior with its teeth and hooves. Above them, the peak of the mountain was a dark shadow that merged with its reflection in the lake, slowly vanishing under the fog.

The warrior felt a sudden nudge on his elbow and whirled around reflexively. His arrow burst from his bow and slammed ineffectually into a nearby tree. The scruffy dog watched the quivering arrow in the tree with interest and then turned to look up at the warrior. Tentatively, it wagged its tail and then sat down and cocked its head.

Tears sprang to the warrior's eyes. He didn't know whether to pat the beast or kill it for leading his children to this place. But it was not the dog's fault. It was his fault. He had not warned his children of the monster Amhuluk. He had not repeated the story of the children who died on the monster's spotted horns. He had not believed the truth of the story until today.

The warrior sank to the ground beside the dog, suddenly exhausted, and patted its shaggy head. "Where are they, boy? Where are my children?" His voice sounded dull and muted in the silence. The dog's tail wagged when he heard the warrior's voice. He glanced at the dark, foggy lake and then trotted up the bank to a grassy knoll. The dog lay down, as if to say, "There is nothing you can do tonight. Wait until morning." The horse followed the dog, turning to look back at his master expressively. The warrior knew the creatures were right. He could not do more in the darkness and the fog. To stay on the dark shore where Amhuluk could reach him while he slept was suicide. He climbed up to the knoll.

The bubble of silence stayed around the warrior as he made a rough camp for the night. He could feel a bit of a breeze, but it made no sound. The fog was a constant companion. His horse cropped grass a yard away, and he could see its silhouette but could not hear it chewing. He fed the dog and himself, knowing he must keep up his strength. Then he wrapped himself in his blanket and stared into the swirling fog. Were his children alive? Where was the monster? What would he tell his wife if they were dead? This was his fault.

The warrior was awakened by a gust of wind and the muffled sound of voices. He jerked upright and stared into the glowing fog. A clear space opened before him, pushing the fog aside to form a bright pathway that descended to the muddy place where his children had dug for roots. As the warrior watched in horror, two figures floated slowly up from the mud. A boy. A girl. Empty eyed. Dripping wet. They looked like flattened silhouettes. The figures were like and yet unlike his beloved children. The warrior's heart pounded painfully against his ribs. The only sound was the wind. Then a boy's voice murmured directly into his ear: "We have changed our bodies." He clapped his hand to the side of his head, his skin goose-fleshed and his body shaking with terror.

The light vanished. The pathway disappeared. Dark fog swirled around his face. The warrior lay panting and shaking until the dog padded over and licked his face. Then he turned over and sobbed in despair. What else could such a vision mean but that his children were dead? Drowned on the horns of Amhuluk the Monster. And it was his fault.

Sound returned with the dawn. The wind rustled the leaves; animals stirred and scurried through the underbrush. Little waves lapped the shore. The horse whinnied and shook its mane. The dog whined for a bit of dried meat, which the grim-faced warrior gave him. He could not eat himself in his grief.

"We must bring their bodies home to their mother," he told the little dog. "It is only fitting. We must find them."

The warrior walked down to the shore with his axe in one hand and his spear in the other, his eyes watchful for two spotted horns the size of small trees. In the growing light, he saw movement to his right where the lake curved away into an unseen inlet. Two paper-thin figures were rising from the water—the dark silhouettes of a boy and a girl. They were empty eyed, and their faces were blank.

AMHULUK THE MONSTER

The warrior braced himself, waiting for the voice in his ear. This time it was a girl who spoke: "We have changed our bodies."

The little dog barked and charged around the lake toward the figures, which vanished instantly. The man followed more slowly, for there was no clear path. The horse trotted behind, glancing nervously from time to time at the rippling waters that held horror beneath their peaceful surface.

When the warrior reached the inlet, he saw the dark silhouettes again, rising from the mud on the shoreline a half mile distant. Two voices chanted: "We have changed our bodies." Then they vanished. The dog raced onward. The warrior grimly marched through brush and bracken, accompanied by the whistling wind in the trees and his horse.

The warrior saw the ghosts two more times as he made his way around the lake. He was opposite the place where he had first emerged from the deer trail when the dog barred his path and his horse reared slightly behind him. A moment later, he saw what had disturbed the animals. A swampy marshland edged the lake in front of him. Rank upon rank of tall reeds filled the space, and masses of lily pads glowed in the sun-sparkled waters. Two spotted trees rose above the swamp, curving up to a point like a pair of massive horns. The marshland was the home of Amhuluk the Monster.

At once, the warrior turned and gestured toward his horse, urging the animal to run away. The animal's eyes rolled once, white with terror. It was torn between its desire to retreat and its desire to stay and protect its beloved master.

"Go, old friend. I will come shortly with the bodies of my children, and you can carry us home," the warrior murmured in its ear. The horse nudged his face, seeming to understand. It backed away silently and made its way to safety farther up the mountain slope. It would await his return.

The warrior gripped his axe in one sweaty palm and his spear in the other. He strode toward the swamp, his eyes fixed on the spotted trees. Within two strides, the wind came howling down from the mountain peak. The waters of the lake grew dim as a massive storm cloud swirled up from nowhere and blacked out the sun. Two children's voices wailed, "We have changed our bodies." Two silhouettes appeared dangling from each of the two spotted horns that lay still and silent in the swamp ahead.

As if awaking in response, the huge head of Amhuluk the Monster rose before the warrior, breaking through the reeds. Its body dripped with lily pads and tangled roots. Its spotted horns seemed to brush the swirling clouds overhead as the monster's glowing red eyes peered down at the warrior, sinuous neck weaving to and fro. The warrior's axe and spear seemed ludicrously insufficient for the task ahead.

The warrior gripped the spear, calculating the best place to throw it. Should he aim for the monster's eye? For its throat? There must be some vulnerable place in that thick hide. But where was it? He would only get one shot.

"Give me the bodies of my children!" he roared. He would try to blind the monster, he decided, rearing back in preparation.

At his feet, the scruffy dog sank to its haunches and howled. The howl was answered immediately from all sides. Every ridge and inlet echoed with the wailing of dogs, growing louder and fiercer every second. The sound was overwhelming. The monster froze in place. The black silhouettes of the boy and girl dangling from each horn swayed back and forth and then stilled. The startled warrior clapped his wrists over his ears, still clutching his weapons. The sound would drive him insane. He swayed beneath the weight of it, staring into the mesmerizing red eyes of Amhuluk the Monster.

The howling ceased abruptly, and a muffling silence clamped around the warrior like a vice. The black clouds swirled, the waves crashed on the shoreline, and the wind howled and battered at the warrior. But he heard nothing save his own breath and a very small voice whispering: "Father? Is that you?"

The warrior turned toward the sound and saw a tattered little girl covered in mud stumbling toward him through a previously unseen trail in the marsh grasses. The monster spotted the escaping child and lowered its sharp horns in preparation for a killing blow. The warrior leapt in front of the girl, raising his axe and spear, prepared to fight to the death to protect his daughter.

Preternatural silence surrounded the warrior as he braced for the attack. He could see the windstorm buffeting the trees and mountaintop and lake. He could feel the earth tremble as the monster charged. But he could hear nothing.

Suddenly, the scruffy dog pushed itself in front of the warrior, standing alone between the charging monster and his master. It flattened its ears and tail and bristled at Amhuluk the Monster. Even through the sound-muffling silence, the warrior heard its menacing growl.

When it saw the scruffy dog, Amhuluk the Monster reared back as if struck, the silhouetted bodies of the children flapping obscenely from its horns. A second later, the warrior felt his daughter's body slam against him, her arms clutching him around the waist in terror.

The warrior heard a second growl and saw the dog's littermate trotting up the swamp path with his younger son in tow. The boy was covered in mud, and his eyes were wide with fear, but he was alive.

Amhuluk the Monster's head swayed, contemplating the two dogs that defied its right to the prizes it had snatched from the lakeshore. Then the monster locked gazes with the warrior. For a timeless moment, the whole world held its breath as they stared at each other. Suddenly the monster blinked its huge red eyes and relaxed its neck. It pulled its horned head up and away from the warrior and his children.

Time sped up and sound returned. The warrior heard the gasp of his young son, the sobs of his daughter, and the growl of the protective dogs. The supernatural storm reversed itself; wind and clouds unfurled themselves and dissipated as suddenly as they had arrived. The warrior's younger son hurtled himself across the remaining yards between them and flung himself against his father and sister.

As the reunited family embraced, the two silhouetted figures floated down from the monster's spotted horns to hover in front of the warrior.

"We have changed our bodies," the girl silhouette said.

"But we have saved theirs," said the boy silhouette.

"Go from this place and do not return," they said together.

They vanished, and Amhuluk the Monster slowly sank beneath the waters of the lake until just the tips of his spotted horns showed over the swampland.

Gathering up his children, the trembling warrior carried them to the place where his horse waited. Behind him, the scruffy dog bared its teeth at the spotted horns, growled a final warning, and then followed his master home.

Resources

Anderson, J. *Horror Stories of Lincoln County*. Eugene: Randall V. Mills Archive of Northwest Folklore at the University of Oregon, 1973.

Asfar, Daniel. *Ghost Stories of America*. Edmonton, AB: Ghost House Books, 2001.

———. *Ghost Stories of the Civil War*. Edmonton, AB: Ghost House Books, 2001.

———. *Haunted Battlefields*. Edmonton, AB: Ghost House Books, 2004.

Bader, Chris. *Strange Northwest*. Blaine, WA: Hancock House Publishers, 1995.

Bakeless, John, ed. *The Journals of Lewis and Clark*. New York: Signet Classics, 2002.

Barlow, Jeffrey, and Christine Richardson. *China Doctor of John Day*. Hillsboro, OR: Binford & Mort Publishing, 1979.

Battle, Kemp P. *Great American Folklore*. New York: Doubleday & Company, Inc., 1986.

Beckham, Stephen Dow. *Tall Tales from the Rogue River*. Corvallis: Oregon State University Press, 1990.

Botkin, B. A., ed. *A Treasury of American Folklore*. New York: Crown, 1944.

Brewer, J. Mason. *American Negro Folklore*. Chicago: Quadrangle Books, 1972.

———. *Dog Ghosts and Other Negro Folk Tales*. Austin: University of Texas Press, 1958.

Brown, D. *Legends*. Eugene: Randall V. Mills Archive of Northwest Folklore at the University of Oregon, 1971.

Brunvand, Jan Harold. *The Choking Doberman and Other Urban Legends*. New York: W. W. Norton, 1984.

————. *The Vanishing Hitchhiker.* New York: W. W. Norton, 1981.

Christensen, Jo-Anne. *Ghost Stories of Texas.* Edmonton, AB: Lone Pine Publishing, 2001.

Clark, Ella E. *Indian Legends of the Pacific Northwest.* Berkley: University of California Press, 1953.

Clason, Leslie D. *Narratives of the Rogue Valley.* Eugene: Randall V. Mills Archive of Northwest Folklore at the University of Oregon, 1984.

Cobb, Todd. *Ghosts of Portland, Oregon.* Atglen, PA: Schiffer Publishing, Ltd., 2008.

Coffin, Tristram P., and Hennig Cohen, eds. *Folklore in America.* New York: Doubleday & AMP, 1966.

————. *Folklore from the Working Folk of America.* New York: Doubleday, 1973.

Cohen, Daniel. *Ghostly Tales of Love & Revenge.* New York: Putnam Publishing Group, 1992.

Cohen, Daniel, and Susan Cohen. *Hauntings & Horrors.* New York: Dutton Children's Books, 2002.

Coleman, Christopher K. *Ghosts and Haunts of the Civil War.* Nashville, TN: Rutledge Hill Press, 1999.

Cornplanter, J. J. *Legends of the Longhouse.* Philadelphia: J. B. Lippincott, 1938.

Costopoulos, Nina. *Lighthouse Ghosts and Legends.* Birmingham, AL: Crane Hill Publishers, 2003.

Dattilio, Daniel J. *Fort Clatsop: The Story Behind the Scenery.* Las Vegas, NV: KC Publications, Inc., 2004.

Davis, Jefferson. *Ghosts and Strange Critters of Washington and Oregon.* Vancouver, WA: Norseman Ventures, 1999.

————. *Ghosts, Critters & Sacred Places of Washington and Oregon.* Vancouver, WA: Norseman Ventures, 1999.

————. *Ghosts, Critters & Sacred Places of Washington and Oregon II.* Vancouver, WA: Norseman Ventures, 2000.

————. *Ghosts, Critters & Sacred Places of Washington and Oregon III.* Vancouver, WA: Norseman Ventures, 2005.

Dorson, R. M. *America in Legend*. New York: Pantheon Books, 1973.

Downer, Deborah L. *Classic American Ghost Stories*. Little Rock, AR: August House Publishers, Inc., 1990.

Dwyer, Jeff. *Ghost Hunter's Guide to Portland and the Oregon Coast*. Gretna, LA: Pelican Publishing Company, Inc., 2015.

Editors of *Life*. *The Life Treasury of American Folklore*. New York: Time Inc., 1961.

Elizabeth, Norma, and Bruce Roberts. *Lighthouse Ghosts*. Birmingham, AL: Crane Hill Publishers, 1999.

Erdoes, Richard, and Alfonso Ortiz. *American Indian Myths and Legends*. New York: Pantheon Books, 1984.

Eufrasio, Al & Jeff Davis. *Weird Oregon*. New York: Sterling Publishing Co., Inc., 2010.

Flanagan, J. T., and A. P. Hudson. *The American Folk Reader*. New York: A. S. Barnes & Co., 1958.

Gatschet, Albert S. "Oregonian Folk-Lore." *Journal of American Folklore* 4, no. 13 (1891): 139–43. DOI: 10,2307/533930.

Hacker, B. *Mr. Floyd Finn*. Eugene: Randall V. Mills Archive of Northwest Folklore at the University of Oregon, 1974.

Hauck, Dennis William. *Haunted Places: The National Directory*. New York: Penguin Books, 1994.

Helm, Mike. *Oregon's Ghosts and Monsters*. Eugene, OR: Rainy Day Press, 1983.

Hildenbrand, D. G. *Supernatural Tales of the Rogue Valley*. Eugene: Randall V. Mills Archive of Northwest Folklore at the University of Oregon, 1973.

Holub, Joan. *The Haunted States of America*. New York: Aladdin Paperbacks, 2001.

Jameson, W. C. *Buried Treasures of the Pacific Northwest*. Little Rock, AR: August House, Inc., 1995.

Jones, Suzi. *Oregon Folklore*. Eugene: University of Oregon and the Oregon Arts Commission, 1977.

Judson, Katherine Berry. *Myths and Legends of the Pacific Northwest: Especially of Washington and Oregon*. Chicago: A. C. McClurg & Co., 1912.

Leach, M. *The Rainbow Book of American Folk Tales and Legends.* New York: The World Publishing Co., 1958.

Leeming, David, and Jake Page. *Myths, Legends, & Folktales of America.* New York: Oxford University Press, 1999.

Little, Gigi, ed. *City of Weird: 30 Otherworldly Portland Tales.* Portland, OR: Forest Avenue Press, 2016.

MacDonald, Margaret Read. *Ghost Stories from the Pacific Northwest.* Little Rock, AR: August House Publishers, Inc., 1995.

Mott, A. S. *Ghost Stories of America, vol. II.* Edmonton, AB: Ghost House Books, 2003.

Murphy, Dan. *Oregon Trail, Voyage of Discover: The Story Behind the Scenery.* Las Vegas, NV: KC Publications, Inc., 1997.

Norman, Michael, and Beth Scott. *Historic Haunted America.* New York: Tor Books, 1995.

Peck, Catherine, ed. *A Treasury of North American Folk Tales.* New York: W. W. Norton, 1998.

Petchell, Daniel. *Treasure Tales of the Oregon Coast.* Bend: Oregon Treasure Publishing, 2005.

Polley, J., ed. *American Folklore and Legend.* New York: Reader's Digest Association, 1978.

Ramsey, Jarold, ed. *Coyote Was Going There.* Seattle: University of Washington Press, 1977.

Reevy, Tony. *Ghost Train!* Lynchburg, VA.: TLC Publishing, 1998.

Roberts, Nancy. *Civil War Ghost Stories & Legends.* Columbia: University of South Carolina Press, 1992.

Rule, Leslie. *Coast to Coast Ghosts.* Kansas City, KS: Andrews McMeel Publishing, 2001.

Schwartz, Alvin. *Scary Stories to Tell in the Dark.* New York: Harper Collins, 1981.

Seaburg, William R., and Pamela T. Amoss, eds. *Badger and Coyote Were Neighbors.* Corvallis: Oregon State University Press, 2000.

Severe, Pam, and Lon Thornburg. *More on the Pendleton Underground.* Bend, OR: Maverick Publications, 2003.

Skinner, Charles M. *American Myths and Legends*, vol. 1. Philadelphia: J. B. Lippincott, 1903.

———. *Myths and Legends of Our Own Land*, vols. 1 & 2. Philadelphia: J. B. Lippincott, 1896.

Smitten, Susan. *Ghost Stories of Oregon*. Auburn, WA: Lone Pine Publishing, 2001.

Spence, Lewis. *North American Indians: Myths and Legends Series*. London: Bracken Books, 1985.

Steward, Donna. *Ghosthunting Oregon*. Cincinnati, OH: Clerisy Press, 2014.

Varney, Phillip. *Ghost Towns of the Pacific Northwest*. St. Paul, MN: Voyageur Press, 2005.

Waggoner, George A. *Stories of Old Oregon*. Whitefish, MT: Kessinger Publishing, 2007.

Weeks, Andy. *Haunted Oregon*. Mechanicsburg, PA: Stackpole Books, 2014.

White, D. *Folk Narratives*. Eugene: Randall V. Mills Archive of Northwest Folklore at the University of Oregon, 1971.

Worchester, Thomas K. *Bunco Kelly and Other Yarns of Portland and Northwest Oregon*. Beaverton, OR: TMS Book Service, 1983.

Yuskavitch, Jim. *Oregon Myths & Legends*. Guilford, CT: TwoDot, 2017.

Zeitlin, Steven J., Amy J. Kotkin, and Holly Cutting Baker. *A Celebration of American Family Folklore*. New York: Pantheon Books, 1982.

About the Author

S. E. Schlosser has been telling stories since she was a child, when games of "let's pretend" quickly built themselves into full-length tales acted out with friends. A graduate of Houghton College, the Institute of Children's Literature, and Rutgers University, she created and maintains the award-winning Web site Americanfolklore.net, where she shares a wealth of stories from all fifty states, some dating back to the origins of America. Sandy spends much of her time answering questions from visitors to the site. Many of her favorite e-mails come from other folklorists who delight in practicing the old tradition of "who can tell the tallest tale."

About the Illustrator

Artist Paul Hoffman trained in painting and printmaking, with his first extensive illustration work on assignment in Egypt, drawing ancient wall reliefs for the University of Chicago. His work graces books of many genres—children's titles, textbooks, short story collections, natural history volumes, and numerous textbooks. For *Spooky Oregon*, he employed a scratchboard technique and an active imagination.